THE ILLUSTRATED ENCYCLOPEDIA OF
MACHINE GUNS

THE ILLUSTRATED ENCYCLOPEDIA OF
MACHINE GUNS

A HISTORY AND DIRECTORY OF MACHINE GUNS FROM THE 19TH CENTURY TO THE PRESENT DAY, SHOWN IN 220 PHOTOGRAPHS

WILL FOWLER & PATRICK SWEENEY

southwater

This edition is published by Southwater,
an imprint of Anness Publishing Ltd,
108 Great Russell Street,
London WC1B 3NA;
info@anness.com

www.southwaterbooks.com; www.annesspublishing.com; twitter: @Anness_Books

Anness Publishing has a new picture agency outlet for images
for publishing, promotions or advertising. Please visit our
website www.practicalpictures.com for more information.

A CIP catalogue record for this book
is available from the British Library.

Designed and produced for Anness Publishing Ltd by
the Bridgewater Book Company Limited.

Publisher: Joanna Lorenz
Senior Editor: Felicity Forster
Project Managers: Sarah Doughty and Cath Senker
Photography: Gary Ombler
Designer: Alistair Plumb
Art Director: Michael Whitehead
Production Controller: Pirong Wang

Previously published as part of a larger volume,
The World Encyclopedia of Rifles and Machine Guns

PUBLISHER'S NOTE
Although the information in this book is believed to be accurate and true at the time of going to press,
neither the authors nor the publisher can accept any legal responsibility or liability for any
errors or omissions that may have been made.

PAGE 1 Maxim M1905 (Russia).
PAGE 2 German grenadier with an MG34.
PAGE 3 MG Browning (China).
BELOW M134 (GAU-2B/A) (USA).
OPPOSITE BREN Mark 1 (Australia).

Contents

Introduction

Firearms have exerted a fascination since medieval times, and today's automatic weapons are more accurate and effective than the first designers could ever have imagined. The machine gun was developed exclusively for major conflict – and it has demonstrated its devastating efficiency time and again.

The Somme

World War I seems almost synonymous with the machine gun. On 1 July 1916, the first day of the Battle of the Somme, German artillery and machine-gun crews hunched behind their Maxim '08s killed or wounded about 60,000 British soldiers as they advanced across no-man's-land.

However, rapid-fire weapons in the shape of multiple-firing flintlocks and muzzle-loaders had existed in the 18th and 19th centuries. The Puckle gun – a sort of large mounted revolver – was introduced in 1718 and was said to have fired 63 shots in seven minutes. In the American Civil War (1861–5), the .50/12mm-calibre Gatling gun (1862) with a reported rate of up to 1,000 rounds per minute (rpm), and the Agar "Coffee Mill" (1860), with a rate

of 120 rpm, were used in some numbers. These guns were followed by other hand-cranked multi-barrelled models such as the Gardner, the Lowell and the Nordenfelt. In the period 1870–90 the British and Russian armies adopted the Gatling gun, while the Royal Navy used three makes – the Gatling, the Gardner and the Nordenfelt.

But none of these weapons was a truly automatic machine gun. All required some form of cranking and/or manipulation; a later model of the Gatling had its barrels rotated by an electric motor. This manipulation, combined with the effect of the recoil, meant that the accuracy of these rapid-firing guns was generally unpredictable. The French and Belgians developed similar weapons – *les mitrailleuses*, the principal product being a 37-barrelled weapon invented in 1870 by Joseph Montigny.

Fully automatic

At the close of the 19th century an American, Hiram Maxim, demonstrated a fully automatic weapon – a machine gun. This weapon would change the character of land warfare and dominate the skies when the first combat aircraft took off in World War I. The machine gun would heavily influence infantry tactics, requiring men to move in short dashes and employ "fire and movement", with the machine gun giving covering fire as rifle-armed soldiers closed with the enemy. As rates of fire increased the infantry would almost become ammunition carriers for the machine gun, advancing with belts or boxes of ammunition.

The GPMG

The inter-war years saw German arms designers learn the lessons of World War I and produce a machine gun that fulfilled the functions of both the long-range Medium Machine Gun (MMG) and the Light Machine Gun (LMG). In the MG34 they created the General-Purpose Machine Gun (GPMG). The United States,

ABOVE The Gardner machine gun looks like a conventional weapon, but it was operated by the crank handle on the right-hand side. Ammunition feed was by single rounds fed in from the top.

Great Britain and the USSR fought World War II with both MMGs and LMGs. The British used the superb Bren LMG, a weapon that was still in service with second-line troops in 1990–91 during the First Gulf War. The staggering volume of fire from the MG34 and 42, respectively 900 and 1,500 rpm, was intimidating but could also be inaccurate. A machine gunner would often aim at an area target and produce a lethal "beaten zone" where falling rounds would make movement very risky.

Modern machine guns, such as the Belgian FN 5.56mm Minimi have become lighter and faster firing. Interestingly, the US electrically powered multi-barrelled M134 Minigun and GAU-19/A Gatling-type weapons incorporate technology first used in the designs of the 1860s. However, this development of a proven technology is not new. The Belgian FN MAG – in service with more than 80 armies across the world – uses the double-feed pawl system and the quick-change barrel that replaced the water jackets and cooling fins developed by the Germans for their superb MG42 machine gun in World War II.

In this book

This book begins with a history section charting the incredibly fast-paced development of machine guns – once that potential had been spotted, arms manufacture exploded into a race of innovation. Next, in the directory section, the history of arms manufacture within each country is briefly introduced, then each weapon entry includes a concise description of the firearm and its key specifications, listed by country and manufacturer. The book will enable enthusiasts to identify machine guns and fully appreciate their unique features, funtionality and designs.

ABOVE The Maxim gun was the world's first true machine gun. For mobility on the battlefield it could be mounted on a light gun carriage, with the crew protected by a shield.

ABOVE When the Allies first encountered the superb German MG42 GPMG in Tunisia in 1943, they were intrigued by the stampings and brazings that were used in its construction – these were intended to speed mass production.

ABOVE An American M1917 Browning water-cooled machine gun with the unusual modification of a carrying handle around the water jacket. This allowed the crew to move the complete weapon short distances.

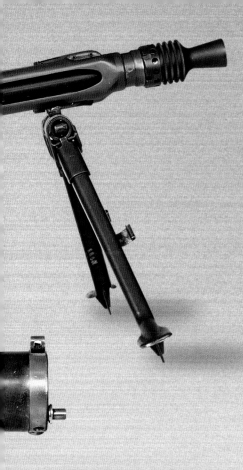

A history of machine guns

The search for a faster rate of fire led to the machine gun, and this crucial weapon will be covered in this section. Interestingly, prior to the demonstration of a recoil-operated belt-fed machine gun by Hiram Maxim, there had been earlier attempts to produce fast-firing weapons.

Heat is the challenge for all automatic weapons designers. It is generated by the exploding cartridges, by the machinery of the weapon and principally by the rounds passing rapidly up the barrel.

If a weapon overheats it will jam or may become a "runaway gun" that keeps firing even though the trigger is not being pressed. The solution for many machine-gun designs was to enclose the barrel in a water jacket; later weapons had barrels that could be changed quickly so that they did not overheat. It was vital for the machine-gun crew to follow the drills for their weapon as conscientiously as a Napoleonic soldier did for his flintlock musket. Skip a drill or fail to complete it properly and the weapon would malfunction.

ABOVE A German 7.92mm Maschinengewehr 08 water-cooled machine gun in a trench system on the Western Front in the latter years of World War I. The gun commander looks for targets while the crew are ready with belted ammunition.

Early multi-shot weapons

The 18th and 19th centuries saw the first multi-shot weapons, such as the English Puckle gun. They were not machine guns, but they pointed to future wars in which heavy volumes of fire could dominate the battlefield. The industrial base of the Union forces in the American Civil War gave inventors the facilities to develop these weapons, notably the multi-barrelled Organ gun and hopper magazine-fed Agar "Coffee Mill".

ABOVE The Puckle gun was a futuristic concept in the early 18th century and, unfortunately for its inventor, James Puckle, as was the case with many innovations, conservative British soldiers and government failed to see its military potential.

Puckle's gun

Born in 1667, James Puckle was an English lawyer, inventor and author. He is credited with two military inventions: a sword of which there is no record and his "portable gun or machine called a defence".

The Puckle gun was a tripod-mounted, single-barrelled flintlock gun fitted with a multi-shot revolving cylinder. At a time when a well-trained soldier could fire three shots a minute from his musket, one man with a Puckle gun could fire nine rounds. In a macabre marketing ploy Puckle offered two versions of the basic design. One gun, intended for use against Christian enemies, fired conventional round balls, while the second weapon, to be used against the Muslim Turks, fired square bullets that were believed to cause more severe wounds.

In 1717, after trials at Woolwich in front of senior officers, the gun was rejected by the British Government. Despite this, Puckle obtained a patent on 15 May 1718, and three years later set up a company to market it. An issue of the *Daily Courant* published in March 1722 carried an advertisement for "Several sizes in Brass and Iron of Mr. Puckle's Machine or Gun, called a Defence . . . at the Workshop thereof, in White-Cross-Alley, Middle Moorfields". At the end of the same month the *London Journal* reported that at a demonstration of one of the guns, "one Man discharged it 63 times in seven Minutes, though all the while Raining; and that it throws off either one large or sixteen Musquet Balls at every discharge with very great Force".

Despite the publicity, Puckle failed to attract backers, and when in 1718 his business went bust, a newspaper of the period ruefully noted that "those are only wounded who hold shares therein".

The 1860 Agar "Coffee Mill"

This is the earliest machine gun known to have been used by the United States Army. Designed by Wilson Agar, it was demonstrated to President Lincoln in 1861, and he was so impressed that he ordered ten at a price of $1,300 a gun; 51 were purchased a year later. They are known to have seen action in a limited number of arenas, and those include the battles of Petersburg, Virginia (1864–5). The machine gun earned its nickname from the hopper magazine feed, which resembled the feed for a coffee grinder. The "Coffee Mill" was mounted on a conventional artillery carriage with a small armour plate to protect the gunner. He had to stand, feeding .58in Minié bullets into the magazine and cranking a handle to fire. The weapon had an effective range of 915m/1,000yd and fired at 120 rpm. The gunner could increase this rate by cranking the handle faster, but because the Agar had only one barrel he ran the risk of overheating it. To obviate this, two spare barrels were always carried with the gun.

Billinghurst-Requa battery

Although the Gatling gun, patented on 4 November 1862, would prove a superior weapon, the Billinghurst-Requa battery, an advanced organ gun patented on 16 September 1862, predates it and is widely regarded as the first "practical" machine gun to be used during the American Civil War. It was the invention of the self-contained metal cartridge that made the organ gun (also known as the volley gun) a practical weapon. The cleverly arranged breech, which closed on a piano hinge, allowed for the ammunition strips to be loaded, fired, extracted, and reloaded quickly by the crew of three.

When the side-mounted loading levers were up, the breech was open. A powder train was laid behind the ammunition strip. Pushing the levers forward secured the breech. A musket cap was placed on the central priming nipple and fired with a simple flip-over hammer mechanism. The barrels, each 700mm/24in long, fired sequentially from the centre out with a characteristic rippling effect.

ABOVE A Billinghurst-Requa battery gun from around 1862. The weight of the 25 musket barrels meant that the gun had to be mounted on a light artillery carriage, and many armies therefore mistakenly considered weapons on gun carriages as light artillery and not a support weapon for the infantry. The idea of a multi-barrelled weapon had first appeared in a design by the Italian Leonardo da Vinci in the late 15th century.

ABOVE The Agar "Coffee Mill" was so-named because the ammunition feed was a hopper that looked very like the one that fitted to a coffee mill. It was hand cranked and capable of 120 rounds a minute.

The Organ gun

Also known as a volley gun or ribaldequin, this was a multi-barrelled gun designed to fire a number of shots simultaneously. Some volley guns could also fire their barrels in sequence. They were not machine guns because they did not load and fire automatically and were restricted by the number of barrels bundled together. The weapon was known as an organ gun because the bank of barrels resembled the pipes in a church organ.

In practice, the large organ guns had little more use than as a cannon firing canister or grapeshot. Mounted on a carriage, they were still as hard to aim and manoeuvre as a cannon, and the many barrels took as long or longer to reload. They also tended to be relatively expensive since they were more complex than a cannon; all the barrels had to be individually maintained, cleaned, loaded and primed. Despite this, the Requa battery, a 25-barrel organ gun, was used by Union forces in 1863 in the American Civil War. A three-man crew could fire seven volleys a minute.

Weapons of war

In the mid-19th century, weapons such as the Gatling were used in action by the Americans in the Civil War, while the French used the Montigny mitrailleuse, one of the first secret weapons, in the Franco-Prussian War. The Swedish-designed Nordenfelt was adopted by the British for use by the Royal Navy.

The Gatling gun

Patented in 1862 by Richard Jordan Gatling, a dentist from North Carolina, this gun was a variation on the revolver principle, with six to ten barrels revolved around a central axis, firing one barrel at a time. The main advantage of having many barrels was that they cooled in between shots, so maintaining their accuracy and preventing "cook-off": the premature ignition of a charge. In 1865 the US Army bought its first Gatling. The first weapons used paper cartridges, but a year later, metallic ones were introduced. Other types of automatic weapons were used in the Civil War but only the Gatling remained in service afterwards.

The Gatling was improved and served with a number of armies around the world as an infantry support or a light artillery weapon. Usually chambered

ABOVE The Gatling gun is one of the iconic weapons of the American Civil War. Soldiers were still unsure whether it was an artillery or infantry weapon, and the wheeled carriage makes it look like a field gun.

for the contemporary general issue rifle cartridge, some naval Gatlings, however, had calibres up to 1in, and some derivatives, such as the Hotchkiss, were up to 2in in calibre. To fire the Gatling, a handle at the back was cranked, which rotated the barrels and fired them in turn. Each barrel had its own bolt that reloaded with each turn. A competent gunner could reach rates of fire of over 200 rounds a minute – a far higher rate than with a single-shot muzzle-loaded or even magazine-fed bolt-action rifle. By 1890, the first true recoil-operated machine guns had been developed but some Gatlings remained in service until 1914.

ABOVE The mitrailleuse used by the French Army in 1870–71 in the Franco-Prussian War was regarded as light artillery even though it used rifle ammunition. Its lethal potential was not fully realized in that war.

The Montigny mitrailleuse

The mitrailleuse was designed in Belgium by Captain T. H. J. Fafschamps in 1851 and manufactured by Joseph Montigny of Fontaine-l'Evêque near Brussels. It was deployed in Belgium in the 1850s, apparently only on a limited basis as a defensive weapon to protect Belgian fortresses.

The Montigny mitrailleuse entered service with the French Army in 1869. Although it looked similar to a modern machine gun, it was strictly speaking a volley-fire gun. It had 26 barrels enclosed in a brass cylinder. A plate pre-loaded with ammunition was inserted into the breach, and to fire it, the gunner cranked a handle. He could fire all 26 barrels in one blast.

At the outbreak of war between France and Prussia in July 1870, the French Army had approximately 190 of these weapons available. Each division was issued with one battery of six guns, issued as replacement for the *Canon de 4* (86.5mm) battery. However, the tactical philosophy behind the deployment of the mitrailleuse was unsuccessful in practice. The guns were ideal at short range against cavalry and infantry, and on one occasion a single mitrailleuse stopped a charge by 500 Prussian cavalry in a murderous 90-second fusillade. Yet French gunners assumed the mitrailleuse was an artillery piece and attempted to use it in long-range duels with very efficient Prussian artillery, a role for which it was entirely unsuited.

The Nordenfelt

This machine gun was of Swedish design and consisted of four to ten barrels mounted on a tripod and fitted with a hopper magazine, with a hand lever to operate the mechanism. It was adopted by the Royal Navy and used as an anti-torpedo boat weapon and by naval landing parties.

There were several designs, including a ten-barrelled Nordenfelt machine gun in .45 calibre, a four-barrelled Nordenfelt 1in-calibre gun with a rate of 200 rpm (introduced into service by the British in 1880, replacing the Gatling .45-calibre machine gun and five-barrelled Gardner machine gun), and the five-barrelled Nordenfelt .45-calibre, 600-rpm gun introduced in 1882.

Torsten W. Nordenfelt

The Swedish engineer Torsten Wilhelm Nordenfelt (1842–1920) teamed up with his fellow countryman and inventor Palmcrantz to produce the M1877 25mm/1in four-barrelled semi-automatic weapon for the Royal Swedish Navy. The gun was gravity fed and fired at 120 rpm. As the Royal Navy was the largest in the world in the late 19th century, Nordenfelt set up a factory in London to supply guns. He teamed up with Maxim to produce guns that were supplied to the Ottoman and German navies. In 1906 the US Navy adopted its first light automatic anti-aircraft gun, the Maxim-Nordenfelt 1 pdr Mark 6.

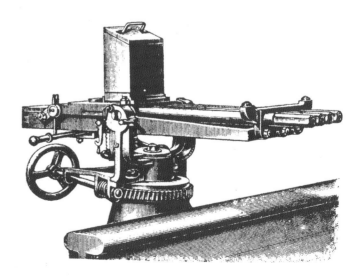

ABOVE The Nordenfelt was produced in several calibres with one to twelve barrels. The weapon shown here is a naval mounting designed to combat torpedo boats.

The first machine guns

Hiram Maxim's invention at the close of the 19th century dominated the 20th century. Colt and Browning, two American small arms giants, combined to produce a machine gun, the Colt-Browning "Potato Digger", while the Danish produced the Madsen – significantly, the first light machine gun (LMG) – which has often been overlooked.

The Maxim machine gun

In 1883–85 US-born Hiram S. Maxim developed the first fully automatic machine gun. After cocking the weapon and pressing the firing button, a round was fired. The recoil energy from firing operated the breech-block; the spent cartridge was expelled, a new round fed into the breech, the firing pin cocked, and a new round fired. As long as the button was depressed a Maxim would fire until the entire ammunition belt was expended. Trials showed that the machine gun could fire 500 rounds per minute. Maxim was knighted for his work after becoming a British citizen.

The Maxim machine gun was adopted by the British Army in 1889. In the following year the Austrian,

ABOVE The Colt-Browning "Potato Digger" received this nickname during the Irish Civil War in 1922, when combatants likened the action of the swinging lever to a farmer digging for potatoes.

German, Italian, Swiss and Russian armies also purchased Maxim's gun. The gun was first used by Britain's colonial forces in the Matabele War in southern Africa, in 1893–4. In one engagement, 50 soldiers fought off 5,000 Matabele warriors with just four Maxim guns.

The success of the Maxim machine gun inspired other inventors. The German Army's Maschinengewehr and the Russian Pulemyot Maxima were both based on Maxim's invention.

The Colt-Browning "Potato Digger"

The 1895/1914 Colt-Browning .3 machine gun was initially adopted by the American Expeditionary Force (AEF) at the start of World War I pending delivery of other weapons, including the Browning M1917. The Colt-Browning, which weighed a little over

ABOVE Under the watchful eye of a British officer and the inventor Hiram Maxim, Henry M. Stanley experiments with a Maxim gun. Unlike earlier weapons the maxim did not require a hand crank and was belt fed.

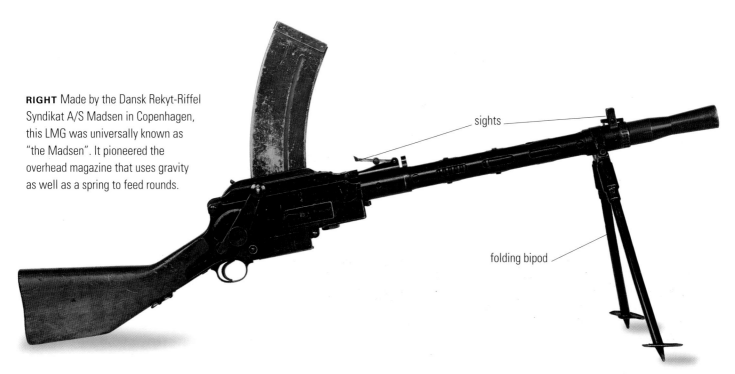

sights

folding bipod

RIGHT Made by the Dansk Rekyt-Riffel Syndikat A/S Madsen in Copenhagen, this LMG was universally known as "the Madsen". It pioneered the overhead magazine that uses gravity as well as a spring to feed rounds.

45.9kg/101lb, had a maximum cyclic belt-fed firing rate of 500 rpm. It is regarded as the first successful gas-operated machine gun, designed by John Moses Browning and offered to the Colt company towards the close of 1890.

Originally designed to use .3 Krag Jorgenson cartridges, the gun was modified in 1914 and chambered for .30/60 cartridges. Italy purchased a number of Colt-Browning 1895/1914 guns in 6.5mm calibre for use by its army as a supplement to the home-grown Fiat-Revelli gun. This machine gun got its nickname "potato digger" because of the action of the swinging lever below the gun.

The Madsen LMG

The Danish 8mm Madsen light machine gun (LMG) was first introduced in 1902 and was the first true light machine gun. A recoil-operated weapon, it was fed from a 20-round curved box magazine. It has been said of the Madsen that the remarkable thing about it was not that it worked well, but that it worked at all. It had a complex mechanism built around the Martini breech-block action. The breech was opened by a recoil-driven cam, and then a separate rammer pushed the cartridge into the chamber before it closed and the round was fired. The Madsen has a long operational history; it first saw action with Russian cavalry squadrons in the Russo–Japanese War of 1904–05. In World War I Germany, Britain and France used it in limited numbers. The German Army formed the first light machine-gun units based on the Madsen; the

Musketen Battalions. They went into action in the Champagne sector in September 1915. Yet the German Army failed to realize their potential. The three Musketen Battalions were used in a defensive role, and so did not demonstrate the advantages of an LMG in the attack. Later, when the utility of an LMG became apparent, the Germans ignored the Madsen and instead developed the MG08/15 water-cooled gun.

Hiram S. Maxim

Born in Sangersville, Maine, USA in 1840, Hiram Maxim became a coachbuilder in an engineering works in Fitchburg, Massachusetts. When he was 26, he obtained the first of many patents for a hair-curling iron. This was rapidly followed by a machine for producing illuminating gas and a locomotive headlamp.

Maxim was employed by the United States Electric Lighting Company as chief engineer and designed a method of producing carbon filaments. At the Paris Electrical Exhibition in 1881 he found the inspiration to develop a machine gun. Maxim moved to London, and in 1884 produced the first working model of an automatic portable machine gun. His Maxim Gun Company, founded the same year, was later absorbed into Vickers Ltd, and he became a director. Maxim was knighted by Queen Victoria in 1901.

Machine gun veterans

Three machine guns that were the cornerstones of infantry operations in World War I – the Russian PM1910, British Vickers MMG and French Hotchkiss M1914 – were still in use during World War II. Indeed, the Vickers was still in use in the mid-1960s, before the British Army switched to 7.62mm NATO calibre ammunition.

The Pulemyot Maxima PM1910

The Russian Pulemyot Maxima na stanke Sokolova (Maxim's machine gun on Sokolov's mount), was also known as the Maxim machine gun 1910 (or Pulemyot Maxima PM1910). This variant of the Maxim machine gun was chambered for the standard Russian 7.62 x 54mm R ammunition. It served as the medium machine gun in the Imperial Russian Army during World War I and the Red Army during World War II. The gun fired at 600 rounds per minute from a 250-round fabric belt. The water-cooling jacket had a screw cap normally fitted to tractor radiators; it was large enough that snow could be packed into the jacket during the bitter Russian winters when all water was frozen. For a degree of mobility, the M1910 could be installed on the wheeled Sokolov mount. By 1943 it was replaced by the excellent SG-43 Gorunov. Maxims were often bolted together on a high-angle mount as anti-aircraft guns.

ABOVE Soviet sailors fighting as infantry in World War II man a triple PM1910 anti-aircraft machine gun. The guns would have put up 1,800 rpm and made an effective low-altitude anti-aircraft system.

ABOVE A sergeant of the British Gloucestershire Regiment, whose ribbons indicate that he is a veteran of World War II, supervises two Vickers MMG detachments in the 1950s in a display of infantry weapons.

The Vickers MMG

The first Vickers machine gun, the Vickers .303in Medium Machine Gun Mark 1, entered service in 1912 and soldiered on with the British Army until 1974. It was a Maxim mechanism that had been inverted and improved. With water in the cooling jacket, the gun weighed 18kg/40lb and the tripod 22kg/48.5lb, while the total weight of the gun was 40.2kg/88.5lb. The Vickers machine gun had a muzzle velocity of 744m/s/2,440ft/s and a rate of fire of 450–500 rpm, and it was fired from a 250-round fabric belt. The introduction of the Mark 8z round added a further 915m/1,000yd to the 550m/3,600yd maximum range. Using a dial sight, which was introduced in 1942, the gun could be used for indirect fire.

During World War I the Vickers MMG gained a reputation as the "Queen of the battlefield" with men of the British Machine Gun Corps (founded in October 1915). It is a measure of the effectiveness and reliability of the weapon that, during the British attack upon High Wood on 24 August 1916, it is estimated that ten Vickers fired in excess of one million rounds over a 12-hour period.

The Hotchkiss M1914

The St Etienne Mle 1907 was the standard machine gun of the French Army at the outbreak of World War I. However, it performed badly in the field. It had so many deficiencies that although guns were captured by the Germans and given the designation 8mm sMG256(f), they were never used, even in fixed fortifications.

There were several modifications until the gas-operated, air-cooled Hotchkiss 8mm M1914 machine gun was produced in 1914, when gas operation was still a relatively new concept. It was a very distinctive gun, with five large circular cooling fins and a metal strip ammunition feed. The Hotchkiss became the French army's standard heavy tripod-mounted MMG in World War I. Twelve divisions of the American Expeditionary Forces (AEF) in France were equipped with the Mle 1914 Hotchkiss in 1917–18.

ABOVE The French mitrailleuse St Etienne Mle 1907 had evolved from the earlier Mle 1905 produced by the State Arsenal Puteaux. It was gradually replaced in service during World War I.

cooling fins

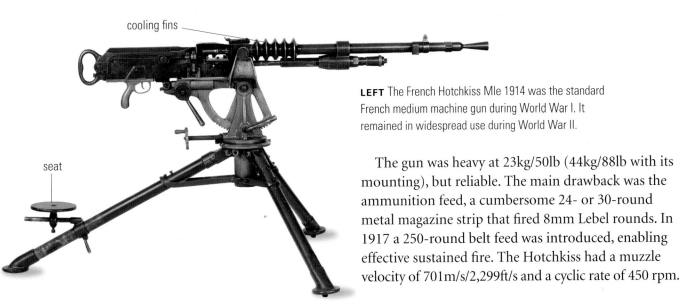

seat

LEFT The French Hotchkiss Mle 1914 was the standard French medium machine gun during World War I. It remained in widespread use during World War II.

The gun was heavy at 23kg/50lb (44kg/88lb with its mounting), but reliable. The main drawback was the ammunition feed, a cumbersome 24- or 30-round metal magazine strip that fired 8mm Lebel rounds. In 1917 a 250-round belt feed was introduced, enabling effective sustained fire. The Hotchkiss had a muzzle velocity of 701m/s/2,299ft/s and a cyclic rate of 450 rpm.

Machine-gun tactics in World War I

In 1914 a German Army battalion had six Maxim MG Modell 1908 machine guns; in contrast, a British battalion had only two Vickers Mark 1s, or Maxims. However, from the outset of the fighting, the Germans tactically concentrated these already co-ordinated battalion teams into batteries and thus gave the appearance, and effect, of having even more machine guns than was actually the case. They gave this impression at Loos, where German machine-gun crews opened fire at 1,400m/1,530yd on the advancing British infantry on the afternoon of

26 September 1915. They inflicted 8,000 casualties (50 per cent) on just two British New Army Divisions (21st and 24th). One German single machine-gun crew is said to have fired 12,500 rounds.

In 1917–18 the British and Germans made a change from the defensive to a more offensive role for the machine gun. The British Machine Gun Corps undertook highly co-ordinated offensive and defensive tactics, including barrages. The infantry then concentrated on the deployment, with much success, of the lighter Lewis machine guns at the platoon level.

The good and the bad

The Italian Fiat-Revelli M1914 must have been a gunner's nightmare, with a complex mechanism that was prone to jamming. The unreliable French Chauchat LMG was designed by three men – Chauchat, Suterre and Riberolle – and as such has been called a gun designed by committee. The American-designed British-built Lewis gun, however, would be one of World War I's success stories.

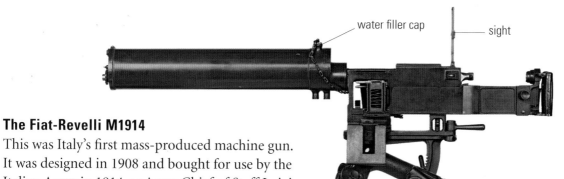

water filler cap

sight

The Fiat-Revelli M1914

This was Italy's first mass-produced machine gun. It was designed in 1908 and bought for use by the Italian Army in 1914, as Army Chief of Staff Luigi Cadorna prepared the Italian Army for its 1915 entry into World War I.

The 6.5mm calibre Fiat-Revelli was water cooled and fired from a 50-round (later 100-round) magazine composed of ten columns of five rounds feeding from the left. Unsurprisingly, given such a loading method, it jammed frequently, but despite this it remained in service for the duration of the war.

It bore a superficial resemblance to both the Maxim and Vickers machine guns but had an entirely different mechanism. Using a delayed blowback mechanism, the barrel and bolt recoiled a short distance, held in place by a swinging wedge. As the

ABOVE The Italian Fiat-Revelli had a complex mechanism, which included a feed system that consisted of a magazine with ten compartments.

latter opened, the bolt was released so that it could be blown back by the spent case's recoil. The overly complex design of this mechanism led to cartridge extraction difficulties; consequently, an oil reservoir was used to lubricate cartridges before they were loaded into the gun. However, oil attracts dirt and dirt can jam mechanisms.

Isaac Newton Lewis

In 1911, a serving American officer and amateur inventor, Colonel Isaac Newton Lewis, perfected a light machine gun originally designed by another American, Samuel Maclean. The American Army showed no interest in its production, so Colonel Lewis retired and moved to Belgium in January 1913, where the Belgians undertook its manufacture. Surprisingly, its calibre was 7.7mm or .303, the calibre of the standard British rifle round.

When Germany invaded Belgium in 1914, the German forces who came up against the weapon called it "the Belgian rattlesnake". Many of Lewis's Belgian workers fled to Britain, where they were given employment by the Birmingham Small Arms Company (BSA), which bought the licence to manufacture the gun. From 1915 it entered service in increasing numbers with the British Army. By 1916 approximately 50,000 had been produced. In 1915 each British battalion on the Western Front had just four Lewis guns, but by 1917 each infantry section boasted its own Lewis gunner and number two, with battalions by now deploying 46 Lewis guns.

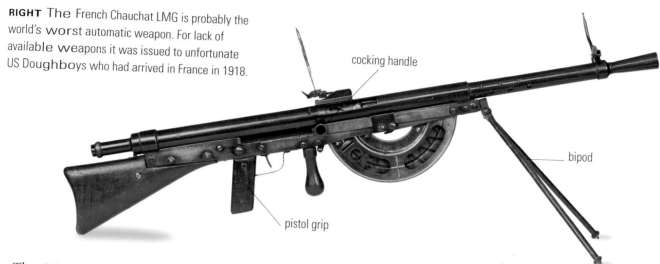

RIGHT The French Chauchat LMG is probably the world's worst automatic weapon. For lack of available weapons it was issued to unfortunate US Doughboys who had arrived in France in 1918.

cocking handle

bipod

pistol grip

The Fiat-Revelli was theoretically capable of firing 400–500 rpm out to 1,500m/1,640yd, but in practice it fired approximately 150–200 rpm. It was modified for use in aircraft in 1915 before British-supplied Vickers and Lewis guns were fitted to Italian aircraft in 1917. The Fiat–Revelli nevertheless held a place within the Italian Army's armoury, albeit with modifications including a 300-round belt feed, until the end of World War II.

The Chauchat LMG

The Chauchat was the light machine gun used principally by the French Army and also by seven other nations, including the USA, during and after World War I. Its formal designation in the French Army was Fusil-Mitrailleur Mle 1915 CSRG. It was also known as the CSRG or Gladiator. More than 260,000 were produced, making it the most widely manufactured automatic weapon of World War I. It was among the first light machine-gun designs of the early 1900s, with

novel features, such as a pistol grip, an in-line stock and select fire lever, that are now standard in modern assault rifles. To speed production it was made from stampings and tubular and lathe-turned components. It fired from a 20-round magazine at 250 rpm and had a rather complex long barrel recoil and gas-assisted mechanism. The Chauchat was designed and built in a hurry during World War I and had numerous faults, and it is recognized today as one of the least reliable automatic weapons ever issued to armed services.

The Lewis LMG

In 1911, Colonel Isaac Lewis of the US Army adapted the complex light machine-gun design of another American engineer, Samuel McLean, and produced the Lewis gun. This early light machine gun was widely adopted by the military forces of Britain and its empire from 1915 onwards. The M1914 air-cooled Lewis gun had a 47-cartridge circular magazine, or a 97-round cartridge for aircraft. The adjustable clockwork recoil spring allowed the gunner to adjust his rate of fire between 500 and 600 rpm, although most gunners preferred to fire short bursts. The gun had adjustable sights and a bipod for firing from the prone position. This gave it an effective range of 600m/655yd.

BELOW Although the Lewis LMG was designed by an American, during the two world wars it became a truly international weapon. Lewis guns accounted for 20 per cent of the Luftwaffe aircraft shot down around London in 1940.

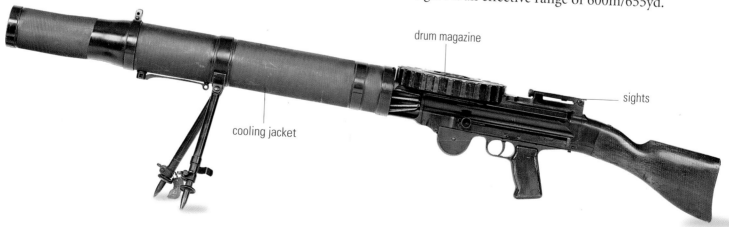

drum magazine

sights

cooling jacket

Old concepts, new designs

Originating from the MG42, the German MG3 machine gun can truly be called an old soldier in the world of small arms design. The Russian RPK-74 is in concept a 7.62mm RPK scaled down to 5.45mm ammunition. The American M60, however, was a machine gun that caused considerable problems and was therefore very unpopular with its users.

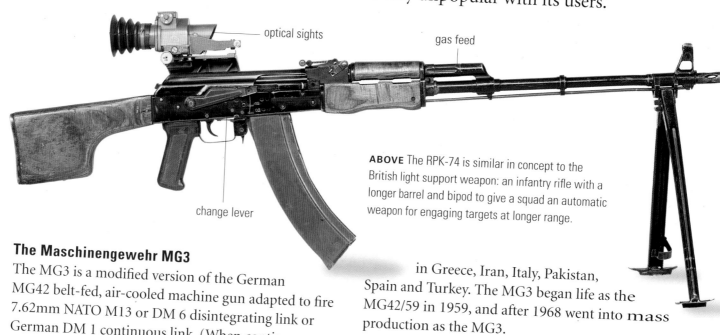

optical sights

gas feed

change lever

ABOVE The RPK-74 is similar in concept to the British light support weapon: an infantry rifle with a longer barrel and bipod to give a squad an automatic weapon for engaging targets at longer range.

The Maschinengewehr MG3

The MG3 is a modified version of the German MG42 belt-fed, air-cooled machine gun adapted to fire 7.62mm NATO M13 or DM 6 disintegrating link or German DM 1 continuous link. (When continuous link has been fired, the empty belt hangs off the gun for reloading later; disintegrating link unclips itself as it is fired.) It is in service in many countries including Chile, Denmark, Saudi Arabia, Norway, Austria and Portugal. The Sarac, an MG3 copy, is built in the former Yugoslavia, and the MG3 is made under licence in Greece, Iran, Italy, Pakistan, Spain and Turkey. The MG3 began life as the MG42/59 in 1959, and after 1968 went into mass production as the MG3.

The MG3 fires from an open bolt and has a short recoil barrel with the bolt locking into the barrel extension via two rollers. Like the MG42, the MG3 has a quick change barrel. The normal drill is to replace it after a 150-round burst. However, in contact this rate can be increased to 200 to 250. As a GPMG the MG3 has a very high rate of fire – between 700 and 1,300 rpm.

The RPK-74

The Soviet Ruchnoi Pulemet Kalashnikova-74, or RPK-74, was developed along with the AK-74 assault rifle as a ten-man squad-level light-support weapon firing the new, small-calibre 5.45mm ammunition. The RPK-74 was adopted by the Soviet Army in the late 1970s and is still in use with the Russian Army today. The RPK-74 has a cyclic rate of 600–650 and a practical rate of 150 rpm. The maximum effective range is 460m/503yd.

LEFT Bundeswehr soldiers with the MG3. The gunner is using the trigger extension grip for the gun's sustained fire mount. The litter of empty cases shows that this post-war clone of the MG42 has a high rate of fire. Its quick-change barrel is replaced after 150 rounds.

Internally the RPK-74 is almost the same as the AK-74 rifle – a select-fire, gas-operated, rotating bolt-locked weapon – but it has a heavier and longer fixed barrel with a bipod, and redesigned buttstock. The RPK-74 can be fed from 45-round box magazines or standard AK-74 30-round magazines. Drum magazines holding 75 rounds similar in design to those of the RPK were also developed. They are much in demand with Russian troops in Chechnya.

Versions of the RPK-74 with a side-mount for the 1LH51 night-vision scopes are called RPK-74N. The first RPK-74s were manufactured with wooden pistol grips and fixed buttstocks, but current guns have polymer grips and side-folding polymer buttstocks.

M60 GPMG

Entering service in the late 1950s, the American M60 GPMG was designed towards the end of the 1940s. Its design drew on a number of German wartime developments including the MG42 machine gun and FG 42 automatic rifle. It had no gas regulator, which sometimes resulted in the gun jamming if fouled or, less usually, in a "runaway gun". This occurred when the working parts went back far enough to feed, chamber and fire a round but not far enough to be engaged by the sear, so that even if the pressure is taken off the trigger the gun keeps on firing. In these conditions the only option is to hold on to the belt to prevent it from feeding.

The M60 can be mounted as a sustained fire gun or on vehicles and has a quick-change barrel and integral bipod. Both the M60 and M60E3 have a cyclic rate of 550 rpm.

ABOVE A grizzled US soldier in Vietnam has belts of 7.62mm ammunition ready for use for his M60, draped over a tree trunk to ensure that they do not foul in the mud on the jungle floor.

The M60 – "The Pig"

The M60 machine gun was a weapon that seemed fine in theory but for soldiers in Vietnam terrible design defects were obvious. The bipod and the gas cylinder were permanently attached to the barrel, so quick barrel changes after firing bursts of 200 rounds proved extremely difficult during a contact. To handle the barrel, the Number 2 on the gun required a heat-protecting mitten, which was often lost on patrol or in a contact. Finally, key components in the operating group, such as the firing pin, were prone to fracturing. Unsurprisingly, the gun came to be known by frustrated soldiers in Vietnam as "the Pig". A lighter version of the gun, designated the M60E3, was subsequently produced but it was actually no great improvement. It did have a non-removable gas cylinder supporting the bipod, and the new barrel had a carrying handle so barrel changes were quicker and easier. However, the new lightened gun was actually less reliable; the light barrel would burn out if 200 to 300 rounds were fired on fully automatic, so it had to be changed after 100 rounds in rapid fire.

Canada

Manufacture of machine guns first began in Canada in 1938 when the Inglis firm signed a contract to manufacture BREN (from BRio/ENfield) guns for both Britain and Canada. Production started in 1940, and by 1943, some 60 per cent of all BREN guns that were being produced came from Inglis.

BREN Mark 2 Conversion

adjustable gas valve

Like so many countries after World War I, when faced with the prospect of converting to the new 7.62mm NATO cartridge, Canada first adapted older designs. Converting the BREN to 7.62mm required only a new bolt, barrel and magazines and it worked well in the new chambering. The most expensive part to make, the receiver, was simply re-marked to show the calibre change. They were only in use from the early 1950s to the early 1960s until replaced by the MAG 58, but were common in Canadian infantry units.

SPECIFICATION	
MANUFACTURER	Inglis
CALIBRE	7.62 x 51mm
MAGAZINE CAPACITY	20
ACTION	Gas operated/tilting lock
TOTAL LENGTH	1,158mm/45.6in
BARREL LENGTH	635mm/25in
WEIGHT UNLOADED	10.51kg/23.18lb

Inglis Experimental

This was a simplified Oerlikon cannon meant for armoured and infantry use. Also known as the "Polsten" (Polish STEN), it was brought to Inglis by Polish engineers fleeing the German invasion. The Inglis was intended to be faster and cheaper to produce. Designed as light tank armament, it quickly became obsolete. Only the Finns found 20mm anti-tank guns transported by infantry to be useful for long. Introduced in 1939, it was quickly outclassed by armour advances, but stayed in service into the 1950s as a direct-fire infantry cannon.

SPECIFICATION	
MANUFACTURER	Inglis
CALIBRE	20mm
MAGAZINE CAPACITY	30
ACTION	Recoil operated
TOTAL LENGTH	2,210mm/87in
BARREL LENGTH	1,397mm/55in
WEIGHT UNLOADED	68kg/150lb

United States

The United States was a power on the world stage before World War I, but the production requirements for World War II turned it into an arms-producing powerhouse, equalled only by the Soviet Union. Every rifle expert selling to the US government had his own machine-gun design.

Stoner 63/Solenoid

The Stoner 63 was designed to be a "one size fits all" weapon by building the components into the desired configuration using a single, multi-purpose receiver as the "building block". In this way, what was an assault rifle could be built as a belt-fed solenoid-fired fixed machine gun for mounting on a helicopter and fired forward. It could also be used as a top-fed BREN clone, or a belt-fed Light Machine Gun (LMG). The Stoner 63 system was used by the USA Navy's Sea, Air and Land (SEALS).

SPECIFICATION	
MANUFACTURER	Cadillac Gage
CALIBRE	5.56 x 45mm
MAGAZINE CAPACITY	Belt-fed
ACTION	Gas operated
TOTAL LENGTH	762mm/30in
BARREL LENGTH	508mm/20in
WEIGHT UNLOADED	5.25kg/11.57lb

Colt M1895

LEFT The Colt gas lever pivots down, and if too close to the ground thrashes the dirt.

The first Browning machine-gun design to go into production, the Colt used a simple gas system. The gas port, which was drilled into the barrel near the muzzle, threw a hinged lever down and the rod linked to it unlocked and forced the bolt back. Apart from this, it was a normal machine gun, with each round extracted backwards from the canvas belt and then fed forward into the chamber. Potentially, a gas-operated machine gun could be lighter than a recoil-operated one and the Colt was much lighter than the Maxim, Vickers and others, even when the water was left out of them. However, if the Colt gun was mounted too low to the ground the "flapper" would chew the earth, earning the nickname "potato digger". Introduced by Colt in 1895 and used in the Spanish-American War, it lasted to 1918, serving as a training and combat machine gun in World War I.

SPECIFICATION

MANUFACTURER Colt
CALIBRE .30-06 & .303 British
MAGAZINE CAPACITY Belt-fed
ACTION Gas operated
TOTAL LENGTH 1,035mm/40.75in
BARREL LENGTH 711mm/28in
WEIGHT UNLOADED 15.87kg/35lb

Benet-Mercie

This was the Hotchkiss light machine gun turned into an automatic rifle. Discarding the tripod for a rather tall bipod, the Benet-Mercié was used in training by the US Army. Between 1900–1914, the US Army owned less than 1,000 machine guns. Between not knowing which was best suited for their needs, and many officers thinking the army did not need machine guns at all, they only bought a few test samples of any one model. The Benet-Mercie was purchased in 1909 and used for training until 1918. It was popular outside the United States as a portable lightweight machine gun.

SPECIFICATION

MANUFACTURER Colt
CALIBRE .30-06
MAGAZINE CAPACITY 24- or 30-round trays
ACTION Gas operated
TOTAL LENGTH 1,232mm/48.5in
BARREL LENGTH 637mm/25.1in
WEIGHT UNLOADED 12.52kg/27.6lb

Browning M1917

water jacket for cooling

trigger and pistol grip

Tasked with designing a new heavy machine gun for the US Army before World War I, John Moses Browning produced this design in record time. Designed as a recoil-operated water-cooled machine gun, it proved so adaptable that in World War II it was all things to all users: a water-cooled, air-cooled, infantry and air service capable machine gun produced in staggering numbers. For decades after World War II it was ubiquitous, found in all conflicts, sometimes on both sides. It was introduced in 1917 and had a service life in some areas beyond the 1960s.

SPECIFICATION

MANUFACTURER Colt
CALIBRE .30-06
MAGAZINE CAPACITY Belt-fed
ACTION Recoil operated
TOTAL LENGTH 978mm/38.5in
BARREL LENGTH 610mm/24in
WEIGHT UNLOADED 14.78kg/32.6lb
  w/o mount

M60

no handle for changing a hot barrel

Developed by the US Army Ordnance as a General-Purpose Machine Gun (GPMG), the M60 incorporated features of several machine guns combined into one weapon. The bolt and barrel had a short service life because the locking lugs would chip, reducing reliability. Once they were chipped, they would gall the barrel cams. It also had a gas system that could be re-assembled in the wrong way (turning it into a single-shot). Production began in 1960 after years of testing and it remained in service until the late 1990s, when the US Marine Corps persuaded the US procurement system to allow MAG 58s for purchase.

SPECIFICATION

MANUFACTURER Maremont Corp.
CALIBRE 7.62mm NATO
MAGAZINE CAPACITY Belt-fed
ACTION Gas operated
TOTAL LENGTH 1,111mm/43.75in
BARREL LENGTH 648mm/25.5in
WEIGHT UNLOADED 10.43kg/23lb

Marlin M1914

This was the version of the Colt/Browning M1895 produced by Marlin between 1914 and 1918. It was purchased by the US Army for training purposes before and during World War I. As with all air-cooled machine guns, it could overheat if not used judiciously. It was made in two versions. While the first was a copy of the Colt/Browning, the second involved improving the "flapper" design of the Colt to a straight piston parallel to the bore, making it better for use in tanks. Early teething problems almost kept it from service.

SPECIFICATION

MANUFACTURER Marlin-Rockwell
CALIBRE .30-06
MAGAZINE CAPACITY Belt-fed
ACTION Gas operated
TOTAL LENGTH 1,028mm/40.5in
BARREL LENGTH 711mm/28in
WEIGHT UNLOADED 14.74kg/32.5lb

Lewis Mark 6 USN

While the US Army was against adopting the Lewis gun, the US Navy was not. Acquired during World War I, the naval Lewis guns served for years in relative obscurity until the navy gunboats on the Yangtze River were attacked in the early years of World War II, before the United States had even entered the war. As local and light defence weapons, they served well on the gunboats, which were shallow-draft vessels cruising up and down the major Chinese rivers, unlikely to face artillery-class weapons. The high quality of manufacture of the Lewis guns kept them in service into the 1930s, when other machine guns would have been scrapped long before. It is shown here with the 47-round pan magazine.

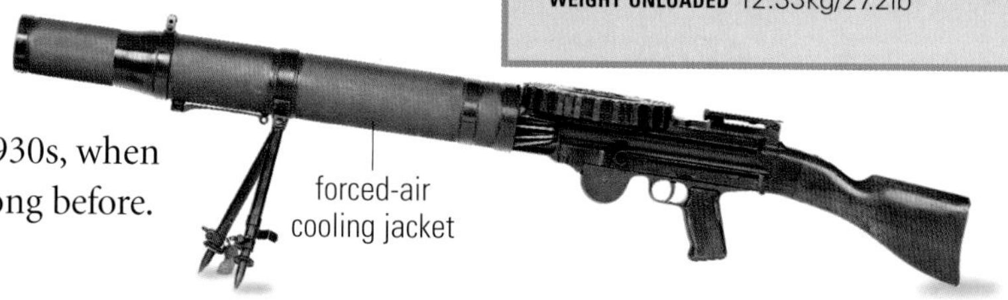

forced-air cooling jacket

SPECIFICATION

MANUFACTURER Savage Arms Corp.
CALIBRE .30-06
MAGAZINE CAPACITY 47- or 96-round drums
ACTION Gas operated
TOTAL LENGTH 1,283mm/50.5in
BARREL LENGTH 668mm/26.3in
WEIGHT UNLOADED 12.33kg/27.2lb

M73

Developed as a replacement in tanks for the Browning and M60, the M73 turned out to be less reliable than the M60 in training and service, and more expensive than the Browning that the United States already had in inventory and wanted to dispose of. One problematic design feature was the barrel-change method: the barrel could be changed from inside the tank, a requirement that made the design complex, expensive and which decreased accuracy and reliability. It was later removed from (limited) service as unfixable and a waste of effort to continue.

SPECIFICATION

MANUFACTURER Springfield
CALIBRE 7.62mm NATO
MAGAZINE CAPACITY Belt-fed
ACTION Recoil, w/gas assist
TOTAL LENGTH 882mm/34.75in
BARREL LENGTH 559mm/22in
WEIGHT UNLOADED 12.70kg/28lb

 Mexico

For a long time, Mexico used imported arms. There were a few designs that Mexican nationals produced, however, and the Mendoza is the most prominent.

Mexico licensed manufacture of the Heckler & Koch 21E as its light and General-Purpose Machine Gun (GPMG). It uses the M2HB as its heavy machine gun.

Mendoza RM2

offset sights

SPECIFICATION

MANUFACTURER Mexico National Armoury
CALIBRE .30-06
MAGAZINE CAPACITY 20
ACTION Gas operated/rotating bolt
TOTAL LENGTH 1,100mm/43.3in
BARREL LENGTH 610mm/24in
WEIGHT UNLOADED 6.39kg/14.1lb

Offset sight
Some say the RM2 was the light machine gun the BAR should have been. A top-mounted magazine needs an offset sight so that the firer can aim.

Designed by Raphael Mendoza, while working for the National Arms Factory in Mexico, the RM2 was a refined version of the M1934. During World War II the US government commissioned more weapons, so Mendoza updated his M-1934, changing the calibre to .30-06 and removing the quick-change barrel feature. The war ended before he could fulfil the contract, and in 1947 he submitted 50 prototypes of the RM2 to the Mexican Marine Corps. The Mexican government declined to purchase any. As Mexican law prohibited the export of "instruments of war" he could not sell it outside Mexico. The M1934 served in the Mexican Army into the late 1950s, but the RM2 ended up in museums around the world.

Chile

Many weapons systems in Chile, large and small, reached the end of their useful life at much the same time. From the mid 1960s, Chile's machine gun needs were filled by

the Rheinmettal MG3 and the FN M2HB. Since the turn of the century, it has been replacing a lot of equipment, from small arms through to frigates and F-16 fighters.

BAR Model 1925

SPECIFICATION

MANUFACTURER Colt
CALIBRE 7.62 x 63mm aka .30-06
MAGAZINE CAPACITY 20
ACTION Gas operated/toggle lock
TOTAL LENGTH 1,214mm/47.8in
BARREL LENGTH 609mm/24in
WEIGHT UNLOADED 8.79kg/19.4lb

Colt was eager to manufacture and export the BAR, as sales had not met expectations. As a result, they could be found in ones and twos in many armouries, both police and military, before World War II. Used as a Light Machine Gun (LMG) in Chilean service, the only problem would have been in keeping the .30-06 ammunition supply separate from the 7.7mm ammunition for the Nambu. After World War II, the US government gave BARs to any ally who asked for them. It was in service from 1918 until the 1960s.

Madsen M1946

Previous Madsen machine guns
purchased by Chile had been in
7 x 57mm. After World War II,
ammunition supply was easiest
in .30-06, the American service cartridge, due to wartime production, and post-
war American Cold War efforts. Chile used the .30-06 until the 1960s, when it
adopted the G3 and MG3, both in 7.62mm NATO, the cartridge easiest to
procure on the world market. It was in service from 1946 to the mid 1950s.

SPECIFICATION	
MANUFACTURER	Dansk Industri Syndikat
CALIBRE	7.62 x 63mm
MAGAZINE CAPACITY	20
ACTION	Recoil operated
TOTAL LENGTH	1,165mm/45.9in
BARREL LENGTH	477mm/18.8in
WEIGHT UNLOADED	9.97kg/22lb

Nambu Type 3, M1920

fins for air-cooling

SPECIFICATION	
MANUFACTURER	Various
CALIBRE	7.7 x 58R
MAGAZINE CAPACITY	24- & 30-round trays
ACTION	Gas operated
TOTAL LENGTH	1,155mm/45.5in
BARREL LENGTH	736mm/29in
WEIGHT UNLOADED	55.33kg/122lb w/tripod

This is one of the many Hotchkiss variants made by Japan. Between the wars,
business was brisk in weapons, and Japan was active on the Pacific coast in
selling. As the Nambu Type 3 was a sturdy, reliable machine gun, the Chilean
Army could not have had any complaints about it other than the weight.
It was produced between 1920 and 1936.

Venezuela

On the Caribbean coast of South America, Venezuelan
forces could count on having to deal with piracy and drug
running. Due to oil exports from 1935, Venezuela has had
the economic reserves to buy modern weapons. After
World War II, they were purchased mostly from FN in
Liège, Belgium. Today, Venezuela makes its own AK rifles.

VZ37

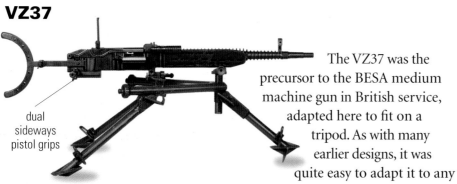

dual
sideways
pistol grips

The VZ37 was the
precursor to the BESA medium
machine gun in British service,
adapted here to fit on a
tripod. As with many
earlier designs, it was
quite easy to adapt it to any
calibre that would fit through the feed tray. For any customer willing to buy,
BRio were happy to modify their products to the national calibre. The VZ37 was
peculiar in that the pistol grip was the cocking handle to charge the weapon: the
gunner would grasp the pistol grip and push forward until it caught the bolt and
then draw it back until it stopped. It was bought from BRio at the start of 1937
and remained in service until the late 1950s.

SPECIFICATION	
MANUFACTURER	CZ, BRio
CALIBRE	7 x 57mm
MAGAZINE CAPACITY	Belt-fed
ACTION	Gas operated
TOTAL LENGTH	1,104mm/43.5in
BARREL LENGTH	678mm/26.7in
WEIGHT UNLOADED	18.96kg/41.8lb

FN M1950

SPECIFICATION

MANUFACTURER FN, Liège

CALIBRE 7 x 57mm

MAGAZINE CAPACITY Belt-fed

ACTION Recoil operated

TOTAL LENGTH 1,041mm/41in

BARREL LENGTH 609mm/24in

WEIGHT UNLOADED 14.06kg/31lb

The Browning machine gun design was as adaptable to other calibres as any. For FN to produce it in 7mm Mauser was therefore straightforward. By 1950, FN had made improvements to the basic Browning machine gun. The sights had been changed, and the barrel jacket was given larger slots for better cooling. The M1950 also features the FN two-bolt mounting system, which FN have used on all machine guns since then. It was produced between 1950 and the 1960s.

Argentina

After World War II, Argentina licensed manufacture of firepower from FN in Liège, Belgium. The success of a proven design such as the Belgian FN MAG 58 meant that it has continued in service. In the Falklands War, both the Argentine and British sides used licensed copies of FN rifles and machine guns.

FN MAG 58

With FN taking over the world's arms markets after World War II, as Mauser had done before World War I, the MAG 58 became nearly ubiquitous. With the adoption of the FAL and MAG 58, Argentina dropped the 7.65mm Mauser cartridge in rifle and machine guns, sold all the older rifles on the surplus market, and adopted the 7.62mm NATO. Observers of the Falklands War commented on how the Argentine and British forces were using identical machine guns. With FN so vigorous in sales and licensing, this has been a regular occurrence since 1958. Argentina adopted the MAG 58 in 1960 and they are still in service today.

SPECIFICATION

MANUFACTURER FN, Liège

CALIBRE 7.62mm NATO

MAGAZINE CAPACITY Disintegrating belt

ACTION Gas operated/toggle lock

TOTAL LENGTH 1,257mm/49.5in

BARREL LENGTH 544mm/21.4in

WEIGHT UNLOADED 10.88kg/24lb

Maxim M1898

long-range sight

firer's seat

SPECIFICATION

MANUFACTURER Simpson & Co.

CALIBRE 7.65mm Mauser

MAGAZINE CAPACITY Cloth belt

ACTION Recoil operated, gas boost

TOTAL LENGTH 1,193mm/47in

BARREL LENGTH 711mm/28in

WEIGHT UNLOADED 29.9kg/66lb w/o water

The Maxim was adaptable to almost any cartridge design, so chambering it for the 7.65mm Mauser was relative child's play for the Simpson & Company manufacturers. Known in North America as "7.65 Argentine", the 7.65 x 53mm cartridge is entirely suitable for military use, although little-adopted and thus not common today. The Maxim M1898 was in use from 1898 to the 1920s, when it was replaced by lighter machine guns.

Brazil

Being cut off from suppliers during both World Wars gave Brazil the impetus to form its own arms industry. Since 1954, Brazil has made sure it is self-sufficient in arms production. Today Mekanika Indutria e Comercio Ltd manufactures the 7.62mm "Uirapuru" for use by the Brazilian Armed Forces.

Madsen M1935

Introduced by Denmark in 1904, the Madsen is the only single-shot rifle action to ever be made into a machine gun. The bolt hinges on a rear pivot pin, in much the same manner as the Martini-Henry rifle. The feed mechanism is activated by a cam shuttling along a track in the side plate and each round is fed down out of the magazine. The Madsen depends on good-quality ammunition, but is essentially low maintenance. In Brazil, the Madsen was used in infantry units and on armoured cars until replaced in the late 1950s by Brazilian-made FALs and MAG 58s.

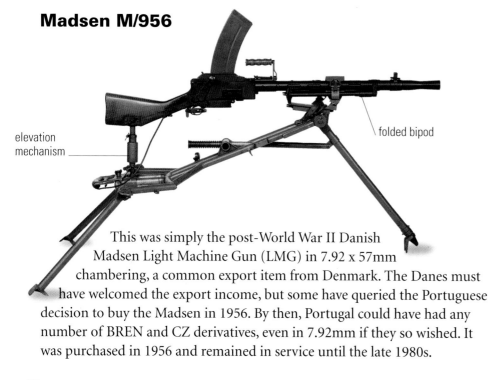

cooling jacket

SPECIFICATION

MANUFACTURER Dansk Industri Syndikat
CALIBRE 7 x 57mm
MAGAZINE CAPACITY 30-round magazine
ACTION Tilting bolt
TOTAL LENGTH 1,165mm/45.9in
BARREL LENGTH 477mm/18.8in
WEIGHT UNLOADED 9.98kg/22lb

Portugal

In World War I, Portuguese infantry fought with France and Britain, equipped with British SMLEs. INDEP, the Portuguese small arms manufacturer now produces a range of weapons under licence, including a copy of the Heckler & Koch-21 light machine gun (LMG).

Madsen M/956

elevation mechanism

folded bipod

This was simply the post-World War II Danish Madsen Light Machine Gun (LMG) in 7.92 x 57mm chambering, a common export item from Denmark. The Danes must have welcomed the export income, but some have queried the Portuguese decision to buy the Madsen in 1956. By then, Portugal could have had any number of BREN and CZ derivatives, even in 7.92mm if they so wished. It was purchased in 1956 and remained in service until the late 1980s.

SPECIFICATION

MANUFACTURER Dansk Industri Syndikat
CALIBRE 7.92 x 57mm
MAGAZINE CAPACITY 30
ACTION Recoil operated
TOTAL LENGTH 1,166mm/45.9in
BARREL LENGTH 477mm/18.8in
WEIGHT UNLOADED 9.97kg/22lb

Reliable long-range fire
Shown here on a sustained-fire tripod, the Madsen was reliable and accurate enough for long-range fire. However, the box magazine limited fire volume, only holding 30 rounds each.

Dreyse M/938

SPECIFICATION

MANUFACTURER RM&M

CALIBRE 7.92 x 57mm

MAGAZINE CAPACITY Belt-fed from drums

ACTION Recoil

TOTAL LENGTH 1,194mm/47in

BARREL LENGTH 622mm/24.5in

WEIGHT UNLOADED 13.15kg/29.2lb

This was a modified Dreyse M1918, used by Germany as the MG13 and sold to Portugal in 1938. A select-fire (rare in an light machine gun) weapon, which can be fired in either semi or full auto settings, it was obsolete even before the Germans sold them. As Portugal was only involved in colonial campaigns, this was not an issue. The Dreyse M/938 was purchased in 1938, but was never used in a conflict, becoming obsolete before ever being accepted. It was a solid and dependable, albeit heavy, machine gun.

Spain

Lacking a major industrial base in the first half of the 20th century, Spain did not enter the world market for machine guns as an exporter. After World War II, Spain followed many other countries and began producing small arms for its own use. CETME currently manufactures the MG3 and the Ameli under licence.

SPECIFICATION

MANUFACTURER Alfa

CALIBRE 7.92 x 57mm

MAGAZINE CAPACITY Belt-fed

ACTION Gas operated

TOTAL LENGTH 1,448mm/57in

BARREL LENGTH 750mm/29.53in

WEIGHT UNLOADED 12.99kg/28.66lb
w/o tripod

Alfa M1944

Lacking access to German small arms (particularly machine guns) during World War II, Spain made its own. The Alfa closely resembled the Italian Breda in layout and function but was certainly a solid medium machine gun. Spain even exported a few to Egypt. The Alfa M1944 remained in service until the 1980s.

CETME Ameli

belt-feed only, no box magazines

Externally a scaled-down MG 42, and internally an HK 21 in 5.56mm instead of 7.62mm NATO, the Ameli has a reputation for being a bit obstinate. Some users report regular malfunctions, while others report flawless reliability. Research suggests that the buffer system may be the main problem and that replacing or rebuilding it turns the Ameli into a spectacularly good Squad Automatic Weapon (SAW). In that role it does not accept the box magazines of any rifle system, only using disintegrating belts. Experience has shown the "feature" of being able to use box magazines far less useful in a SAW than designers had thought. Given the fierce competition from other makers and their designs, the initial problems of the Ameli kept it from gaining market share. The CETME Ameli has been in service since 1982.

SPECIFICATION

MANUFACTURER CETME

CALIBRE 5.56 x 45mm

MAGAZINE CAPACITY Belt-fed

ACTION Roller-delayed blowback

TOTAL LENGTH 900mm/35.43in

BARREL LENGTH 400mm/15.74in

WEIGHT UNLOADED 5.3kg/11.68lb

United Kingdom

The British Army did not take machine guns in any numbers before World War I. But the high rate of fire of British-trained riflemen during the conflict led the Germans to under-estimate the number of machine guns in the British Army. After using one of the heaviest rifle-calibre machine guns (Vickers), after the war Britain adopted the BREN, one of best lightweight rifle-calibre squad automatic weapons (SAWs) ever made.

BESA Mark 2

sliding the pistol grip forward and back cocked the BESA

Developed from the Czech ZB53, the BESA served as armament on tanks. The BESA fired its cartridge while the barrel was moving forward. Thus, part of the recoil was used up in stopping the forward travel of the barrel. This compact design made it useful in the crowded environment of tanks. The design was not changed from the Czech in 7.92mm as the Royal Armoured Corps had its own supply system, separate from that of the Infantry. It was deemed easier to produce and ship 7.92mm ammunition for the tanks than to re-design the BESA to use .303 ammunition. The War Office signed a contract with BRio for licensed manufacture of the BESA in 1936, placing their first order in 1938. They stayed in regular service until 1945, but new tank designs received the L7A1 after the war.

SPECIFICATION

MANUFACTURER BSA
CALIBRE 7.92mm Mauser
MAGAZINE CAPACITY Belts, cloth or disintegrating
ACTION Gas operated
TOTAL LENGTH 1,105mm/43.5in
BARREL LENGTH 736mm/29in
WEIGHT UNLOADED 21.7kg/48lb

Colt M1914

Like the earlier 1895 Colt, this was called the "potato digger" due to the front actuating arm, and was a refined M1895, designed by John Moses Browning. Gas bled off the barrel and pivoted the actuator down. If the gun was too close to the ground, it would dig into the soil. Despite being air-cooled, the Colt had a good reputation for reliability and volume of fire. The slow cyclic rate (400 rpm) kept it cooler than other air-cooled machine guns. Despite its heavier barrel, the loss of the water and jacket made it lighter and more compact than the Vickers or Maxim, and popular with the troops. It was first used in American service in Cuba, but not kept after 1918.

SPECIFICATION

MANUFACTURER Colt
CALIBRE .30-06, .303 British, 7 x 57mm, 7.65 x 54mm
MAGAZINE CAPACITY Belt-fed
ACTION Gas operated
TOTAL LENGTH 1,035mm/40.75in
BARREL LENGTH 711mm/28in
WEIGHT UNLOADED 15.9kg/35lb

Browning Mark 2, Air Service

SPECIFICATION

MANUFACTURER Colt
CALIBRE .303 British
MAGAZINE CAPACITY Belt-fed
ACTION Recoil operated
TOTAL LENGTH 978mm/38.5in
BARREL LENGTH 610mm/24in
WEIGHT UNLOADED 14kg/31lb

The Browning is easily converted from one rifle calibre to another. As long as the cartridge length and rim diameter fit the receiver, the rest of the conversion job is simply detail. Thus, converting Browning machine guns from the American .30-06 to .303 British was easy. Britain purchased many Browning machine guns for air service to arm World War II aircraft. The cyclic rate on aircraft guns was typically increased, with hydraulic buffers and modified springs, from 500 rpm to 1,000 rpm. These guns were quite popular for infantry use. While .303 weapons were desired in 1940, within a few years all aircraft machine guns were .50 BMG.

Browning 1919 A4 conversion

Given the durability, near-ubiquity and availability of spare parts for the Browning .30 machine guns in all their guises, it was no wonder than many countries sought to convert them. When NATO switched to the 7.62 x 51mm cartridge, it was easy enough to convert Brownings of all types to the new cartridge. Some conversions even went so far as to change the Browning from cloth to disintegrating belts. However, as soon as the new generation of general-purpose machine guns (GPMGs) were fielded, with their quick-change barrels, all the old Brownings went back into storage and were subsequently scrapped. However, between the adoption of the T65 (7.62mm NATO cartridge) in 1953 and the manufacture of increasing numbers of the Enfield L7A1, it was a machine gun in any inventory, including British.

BREN Mark 2

A joint development between BRio and Enfield, the BREN gun (a combination of the initials of BRio and Enfield) was adopted in 1937, when production for British use began in Enfield. Experience in World War I had shown that machine guns were an essential part of winning a war, and that troops simply could not move water-cooled guns fast enough to take advantage of any successful attack or breakthrough. The BREN fired from magazines, requiring assistant gunners to keep them fed. But the quick-change barrel allowed a BREN gunner to maintain a substantial rate of fire, for as long as cool barrels were available. The BREN was superbly accurate. In the 1950s many armies converted BRENS to 7.62mm NATO for continued use. From .303 in 1935 to 7.62mm NATO during the 1950s, the BREN was very popular with troops.

top-mounted magazine

carry handle, also barrel-change handle

L7A1

quick-change barrel

This was the Enfield-produced version of the MAG 58. It was also manufactured in variants for tank use and tested as a fixed-mount aircraft machine gun. The L7A1 went on to aerial service in helicopters, where door gunners could use them to protect the aircraft during landings and takeoffs. It found its way into every infantry, marine and airborne unit as well as coastal craft. Other than the Enfield and British-service markings, it does not differ from the FN version. It was adopted in 1959 and is still in use.

L86A2 HK

The L86A2 Squad
Automatic Weapon (SAW) proved
as unreliable as the L85A2 individual
weapon. Heckler & Koch undertook an upgrade but they were not successful:
the L86A2 had the same tactical shortcomings as all other SAWs with only a
magazine feed (no belt-feed, thus low sustained fire) and a barrel that was non-
interchangeable (limited firepower and fast overheating). The longer barrel gave
it more reliability than the similarly upgraded rifle. It was first issued in 1986.

long barrel,
but not quick-change

SPECIFICATION

MANUFACTURER Enfield

CALIBRE 5.56 x 45mm

MAGAZINE CAPACITY 30

ACTION Gas operated

TOTAL LENGTH 900mm/35.43in

BARREL LENGTH 646mm/25.43in

WEIGHT UNLOADED 7.3kg/16.1lb

Rexer (Madsen)

The Rexer machine gun company made
Madsen light machine guns under
licence from Dansk Syndikat until
legal difficulties caused Rexer to
close their doors in 1910.
They managed to fulfil small
contracts to Natal, South Africa, and the Indian Army. Except for the
markings Rexer machine guns are Madsens, and any user familiar with a
Danish Madsen would have no problem using a Rexer.

SPECIFICATION

MANUFACTURER Rexer

CALIBRE .303 British

MAGAZINE CAPACITY 30

ACTION Gas operated

TOTAL LENGTH 1,165mm/45.9in

BARREL LENGTH 478mm/18.8in

WEIGHT UNLOADED 10kg/22lb

Lewis Mark 1

Arguably the best air-cooled light
machine gun of World War I, the
Lewis was used both as an aircraft
gun (fixed and flexible) and an infantry support weapon. Designed in the United
States and initially made there and in Belgium, the Lewis ended up being built
in quantity at BSA. Nicknamed "The Belgian Rattlesnake" by the Germans in
World War I, it was a complex and costly weapon, but very reliable. The pan
magazines were high-capacity, without belts to cause feeding problems. It was
not widely used after World War I, so its service life was from 1914 to 1918.

SPECIFICATION

MANUFACTURER Savage, FN, BSA

CALIBRE .303 British

MAGAZINE CAPACITY 47- or 96-round drum

ACTION Gas operated

TOTAL LENGTH 1,282mm/50.5in

BARREL LENGTH 668mm/26.3in

WEIGHT UNLOADED 12.33kg/27.2lb

Vickers No. 1 Mark 1, Air Service

A gas-operated Vickers (noted in inventory
as VGO), the No. 1 Mark 1 was intended as a defensive
weapon on observation planes and bombers. It had a
fairly high cyclic rate, 950 rpm. When the Browning machine gun was chosen for
that role, the Vickers went off to the Long Range Desert Group of the SAS. There,
mounted four or five to a jeep, they were used by scouts looking for the German
and Italians. With two or three jeeps positioned to bring all their guns to bear in
an ambush, the scouts could fire as many as 1,500 rounds in just over six seconds.
The weapons were declared obsolete and scrapped at the end of World War II.

SPECIFICATION

MANUFACTURER Vickers

CALIBRE .303 British

MAGAZINE CAPACITY 60- & 100-round drums

ACTION Gas operated/rotating bolt

TOTAL LENGTH 1,016mm/40in

BARREL LENGTH 508mm/20in

WEIGHT UNLOADED 8.8kg/19.75lb

France

From adopting the Hotchkiss, its first machine gun in 1897, France quickly settled for designs of limited usefulness and consequently suffered in World War I. Using mainly air-cooled machine guns, French troops could not maintain the sustained fire of the Germans, without assembling larger numbers of machine guns. Larger numbers of troops and guns simply meant larger targets for counter-battery machine gun and artillery fire.

Chauchat (CSRG) M1915

SPECIFICATION

MANUFACTURER Bayonne, others
CALIBRE 8mm Lebel
MAGAZINE CAPACITY 20 rounds
ACTION Recoil operated
TOTAL LENGTH 1,143mm/45in
BARREL LENGTH 470mm/18.5in
WEIGHT UNLOADED 8.6kg/19lb

curved magazine for rimmed cartridges

This is a long-recoil design, where the bolt and barrel recoil together down the length of the receiver, then reciprocate forward separately, the barrel first, followed by the bolt. The basic principle was first designed by John Browning and made in the Auto-5 shotgun. In a rifle calibre the parts have to travel a longer distance to avoid harsh internal impact and battering. It was made in massive numbers during World War I, where it was used as a portable, squad-level firepower weapon in trench warfare. The workmanship is at times quite rough, but the weapon was reasonably reliable, at least in 8mm Lebel.

M1931A

SPECIFICATION

MANUFACTURER Bayonne
CALIBRE 7.5mm French M1929
MAGAZINE CAPACITY 36-round magazine and 100-round drum
ACTION Gas operated
TOTAL LENGTH 1,028mm/40.5in
BARREL LENGTH 596mm/23.5in
WEIGHT UNLOADED 12.47kg/27.5lb

This was a tank and fortress gun pressed into service as an infantry weapon after World War II due to a lack of otherwise suitable machine guns. It was replaced by the AAT-52. The M1931A was unsuited as an infantry weapon for several reasons: it lacked a mechanical safety and fired from an open bolt. When unloading, a round would be left in the feed tray, and unless the operating rod was cycled again after removal of the magazine, it would fire a round even after it had been "unloaded". As a fortress gun, it served from 1931 to 1940. As a stop-gap infantry weapon, it was used until the late 1940s.

AAT-52

SPECIFICATION

MANUFACTURER Bayonne
CALIBRE 7.5mm French M1929
MAGAZINE CAPACITY Belt-fed
ACTION Delayed blowback
TOTAL LENGTH 1,166mm/45.9in
BARREL LENGTH 490mm/19.3in light, 600mm/23.6in heavy
WEIGHT UNLOADED 9.8kg/21.7lb light barrel, 10.6kg/23.38lb w/heavy barrel

Made as a General-Purpose Machine Gun (GPMG), the 52 is an amalgam of the MG 42 feed system and a variant of the CETME/Heckler & Koch roller-delayed blowback. With a light barrel and bipod, it is light enough to almost be a Squad Automatic Weapon (SAW). With the heavy barrel and tripod it is suitable as a heavy machine gun. The ejection is rough on empties, extracting them early in the firing cycle and making them unsuitable for reloading. Mangled brass is not usually a problem in military service, except that in the AAT-52 the metal is so abused it is sometimes ripped in half, causing a malfunction. Despite this, it served from 1953 to the late 1950s, when replaced by the AA F-1.

AA F-1

The AAT-52 was chambered in 7.62mm NATO, and used a French adapter to fit the US M2 tripod. Despite the change in chambering it was still harsh on the extracted and ejected brass, and prone to breaking it. To ease extraction and hopefully prevent broken cases leading to malfunctions, troops oiled the belt as it was feeding, but this could create other problems: the oil attracted dust, dirt and other debris, which was then fed into the mechanism. The Mod AA F-1 has been in service from the late 1950s to the present day.

SPECIFICATION

MANUFACTURER Bayonne
CALIBRE 7.62mm NATO
MAGAZINE CAPACITY Belt-fed
ACTION Delayed blowback
TOTAL LENGTH 1,166mm/45.9in
BARREL LENGTH 490mm/19.3in light, 600mm/23.6in heavy
WEIGHT UNLOADED 9.8kg/21.7lb light barrel, 10.55kg/23.38lb w/heavy barrel

Hotchkiss M1914

An updated version of earlier designs, primarily the M1900, the M1914 was the primary machine gun of France in World War I, and was still in service at the beginning of World War II. It was a reliable, if bulky and heavy, air-cooled machine gun. The feed system used stamped steel or brass strips, each holding 24 or 30 rounds. The strips could be linked by the assistant gunner as the weapon fired, to provide continuous fire. In the sustained fire of trench warfare, the barrel would glow red-hot but the Hotchkiss would still work. Once overheated, it had to be left to cool as the barrels could not be changed while hot. Hotchkiss machine guns with worn barrels had to be sent back to rear areas for a new barrel. Production commenced in 1914, and lasted through to 1918, while the weapon itself remained in service until 1940.

SPECIFICATION

MANUFACTURER Hotchkiss et Cie
CALIBRE 8mm Lebel
MAGAZINE CAPACITY 24- & 30-round trays
ACTION Gas operated
TOTAL LENGTH 1,270mm/50in
BARREL LENGTH 775mm/30.5in
WEIGHT UNLOADED 23.56kg/52lb w/o tripod, which added 27.2kg/60lb

The Hotchkiss designs
The Hotchkiss machine guns were based on a design by Captain Baron A. Odkolek von Augeza of Vienna in Austria.

Chatellerault M1924/29

This was the French answer between the wars to the squad need for firepower. The original M24 was chambered in the 7.5mm 1924 cartridge. When the cartridge was redesigned and shortened in 1929, the old machine guns were rebuilt and the old and new alike were known as M1924/29. It had selective-fire, with the front trigger for semi- and the rear for full-auto fire. The M1924/29 was robust, reliable and popular with the troops. Manufactured from 1924 to 1940, it is still found in use in former French colonies. During the occupation, the Germans did not make any for their use, which is surprising. They would have done well to switch it to 7.92mm and produce it as quickly as possible. However, they did use it to arm their occupation troops, thus freeing other weapons for use on the Eastern Front. It was used by the French Army after World War II into the late 1950s.

dual triggers for full and semi-fire

SPECIFICATION

MANUFACTURER MAC
CALIBRE 7.5 French M1929
MAGAZINE CAPACITY 25 rounds
ACTION Gas operated/linked bolt
TOTAL LENGTH 1,082mm/42.6in
BARREL LENGTH 500mm/19.7in
WEIGHT UNLOADED 11.1kg/24.51lb

St Etienne M1907

action spring around barrel was prone to over-heating

SPECIFICATION

MANUFACTURER St Etienne
CALIBRE 8mm Lebel
MAGAZINE CAPACITY 24 & 30 round strips
ACTION Blow-forward/rack-and-pinion
TOTAL LENGTH 1,180mm/46.45in
BARREL LENGTH 710mm/27.95in
WEIGHT UNLOADED 25.73kg/56.7lb

In a contest of "worst machine gun ever made" the St Etienne is a definite finalist. The action is blow-forward, with the barrel going forward as the action cycles and the bolt (via a rack-and-pinion system) going backwards. While no doubt a design achievement and engineering tour de force, such extra complexity is always bad in a combat arm. The action spring is coiled around the barrel and if the barrel overheats, as it is sure to do in combat conditions, the spring suffers and eventually fails. Despite the urgent need for machine guns in World War I, the St Etienne was so bad it was removed from service and shipped to the colonies.

SPECIFICATION

MANUFACTURER Unk
CALIBRE 13.2 x 99mm
MAGAZINE CAPACITY 20-round strips
ACTION Gas operated
TOTAL LENGTH 1,371mm/54in
BARREL LENGTH 686mm/27in
WEIGHT UNLOADED 20.4kg/45lb

Hotchkiss

Developed between World War I and II, the design was licensed to Japan. The basic Hotchkiss design, while suitable for rifle-calibre cartridges, was strained when it was used in something so large. Curiously, while Hotchkiss was more than happy to license the design to the Japanese, the French Army saw no need for it. In Japanese service it lasted from the late 1930s to 1945. It did not see service in France.

Belgium

With the establishment of Fabrique Nationale (FN) Belgium was well suited to not only equip its own armed forces, but the world's as well. It has succeeded in this task. The Falklands War was not the only conflict waged where both sides used variants (or even identical versions) of FN weapons.

Hotchkiss

anti-aircraft tripod

SPECIFICATION

MANUFACTURER FN, Liège
CALIBRE 8mm Lebel, 6.5 Jap, .30-06, .303 British
MAGAZINE CAPACITY 24- or 30-round trays
ACTION Gas operated
TOTAL LENGTH 1,310mm/51.6in
BARREL LENGTH 787mm/31in
WEIGHT UNLOADED 25.26kg/55.7lb

The Hotchkiss was one of the first air-cooled machine guns. Early models used water to cool the barrel, as long bursts could quickly take it to red-hot. The Hotchkiss used cooling fins to partially deal with the heat produced. One peculiarity of the Hotchkiss was the feed mechanism: metal trays. Cloth belts were viewed as a necessary but awkward feed method, but they had drawbacks. The Hotchkiss trays could not rot or stretch. If they froze, they would still work. The assistant gunner could hook each tray on to the end of the feeding one, to keep up a continuous rate of fire, until the ammunition was exhausted or the barrel finally succumbed to the heat. It was made for export before World War I and used from 1896 to 1914, when the Liège plant was overrun.

Hotchkiss Export Model

odd-shaped but comfortable stock

The Export, also known as the Portative, as well as the M1909, was the Hotchkiss effort at a light machine gun. The locking system was changed to make the weapon more compact, and combined with a reshaped receiver, the weight loss was impressive. So popular as a portable weapon, it even saw use as a Cavalry weapon. The Portative was known in the US as the Benet-Mercie Machine Rifle. The Export could still be found in armoury reserves in 1939, when it was hauled out for yet another war. By 1945 it had been replaced by the BREN and BAR, and fell out of use.

SPECIFICATION

MANUFACTURER Hotchkiss
CALIBRE 8 x 50R Lebel, .30-06
MAGAZINE CAPACITY 30-round tray
ACTION Gas operated
TOTAL LENGTH 1,187mm/46.75in
BARREL LENGTH 597mm/23.50in
WEIGHT UNLOADED 12.25kg/27lb

FN Browning BAR D

quick-change barrel

In an effort to end the stalemate of trench warfare, the US Army intended to introduce massive firepower into the hands of the infantry. One approach was the Pedersen device, which proved a failure. The other was the BAR, which was not. A select-fire rifle-cartridge weapon that could be carried and used by one man, it proved rugged, accurate, reliable and long-lived. The FN Model D differed from the American version in having a finned barrel for greater cooling, and a pistol grip. As an export weapon, it could be made in any cartridge that fitted the basic BAR platform, and has been seen in eight different chamberings. Many armies had the BAR as their machine gun, a Squad Automatic Weapon (SAW). FN sold a great many between the wars and after World War II, until it developed the FAL and MAG 58. It was a standard export item from the 1920s to 1940, and then again in the early 1950s.

SPECIFICATION

MANUFACTURER FN, Liège
CALIBRE .30-06, 7.92, 7.65, 6.5 x 55
MAGAZINE CAPACITY 20-round magazines
ACTION Gas operated/toggle action
TOTAL LENGTH 1,194mm/47in
BARREL LENGTH 606mm/24in
WEIGHT UNLOADED 8.93kg/19.7lb

M2HB

anti-aircraft shooter's brace

When tanks appeared on the battlefields of World War I, none of the armies involved had the means to deal with them. Artillery was too cumbersome, and rifle and machine guns mostly ineffective. John Moses Browning scaled up both his belt-fed machine gun and the .30-06 cartridge, and produced the .50 calibre M2. The war ended before it could be used on the Western Front, but the M2 has been used ever since. The HB is for "heavy barrel", a thicker-walled and heavier barrel than the original, to do away with the weight of a water-filled cooling jacket. Later FN improvements included a quick-change barrel that did not require adjustment on installation. For over a generation the US Army has been trying to replace the M2HB with something lighter, but all efforts have failed to produce any weapon as rugged, versatile and powerful. Production began in 1946 and continues today.

SPECIFICATION

MANUFACTURER FN, Liège
CALIBRE .50 BMG
MAGAZINE CAPACITY Belt-fed
ACTION Recoil operated
TOTAL LENGTH 1,656mm/65.2in
BARREL LENGTH 1,143mm/45.0in
WEIGHT UNLOADED 38.10kg/84lb

FN MAG

SPECIFICATION

MANUFACTURER FN, Liège

CALIBRE 7.62 x 51mm

MAGAZINE CAPACITY Belt-fed

ACTION Gas operated/toggle lock

TOTAL LENGTH 1,260mm/49.60in

BARREL LENGTH 545mm/21.45in

WEIGHT UNLOADED 12.0kg/26.45lb

Designed in the 1950s, the Mitrailleuse d'Appui General (MAG) was meant to be a truly General-Purpose Machine Gun (GPMG), with variants for ground, vehicle and aircraft use. It is an amalgam of designs: a Maxim/Browning-type receiver of riveted plates, the Browning BAR-style bolt as the action and an MG 42 feed mechanism to advance the belt and feed the rounds. It has become near-ubiquitous, and even adopted by the US Army and Marine Corps, replacing the American-designed M60. It is air-cooled, has two settings for the cyclic rate and a quick-change barrel.

FN Minimi

Almost from the moment of reluctantly adopting the 5.56mm cartridge, the US Army sought to replace it. One avenue explored was to find a Squad Automatic Weapon (SAW) that needed something other than the 5.56mm.

SPECIFICATION

MANUFACTURER FN, Liège

CALIBRE 5.56 x 45mm

MAGAZINE CAPACITY Belt and 30-round magazines

ACTION Gas operated/rotating bolt

TOTAL LENGTH 1,040mm/40.94in

BARREL LENGTH 465mm/18.3in

WEIGHT UNLOADED 7.1kg/15.65lb

After 15 years of experimentation and design dead-ends, the army gave up and adopted the FN Minimi, a 5.56mm SAW that used either belts or M16 magazines. The US Army could not simply adopt it, it had to "improve" it, though such endeavours were in fact digressions. The Minimi is now an integral part of many armies at the squad level, where a General-Purpose Machine Gun (GPMG) and the ammunition it consumes would be too heavy. FN sells or licenses the original, not a US Army-improved version. The Minimi, unlike many earlier light machine guns, can be mounted in a tripod as well as used on a bipod. It was introduced in 1982 and is now found worldwide.

Netherlands

The Netherlands adopted the Schwarzlose in 7.92mm rimmed before World War I, opting for a lighter machine gun after the war. Lacking an armoury or manufacturer of their own has not kept the Netherlands from adopting the best rifles and machine guns to be found. They currently field the Minimi and FN MAG.

Lewis M20

96-round drum

SPECIFICATION

MANUFACTURER FN, Liège

CALIBRE 6.5 x 53R

MAGAZINE CAPACITY 47 or 96

ACTION Gas operated

TOTAL LENGTH 1,283mm/50.5in

BARREL LENGTH 660mm/26in

WEIGHT UNLOADED 12.24kg/27lb

Adopted in 1920, the Lewis gun had already proven its worth. Light, handy and reliable, albeit requiring maintenance, the Lewis served as well as any other. The Lewis was adaptable to many cartridges due to its pan magazine. Modifying the design to use the 6.5 x 53R cartridge probably did not take more than a day for the engineers. With proper maintenance, the Lewis worked under even extreme conditions, and continued to do so. It was in use from 1920 to 1940.

HK11

Unlike the HK21, which
was designed for both belt and
magazines, the HK11 was a
magazine-fed-only light machine gun. It was to be an improved and updated
BAR or BREN for use by the West German Army and for export. However, in
the Squad Automatic Weapon (SAW), the trend quickly moved from full-power
machine guns of limited capacity to smaller calibres and larger ammunition
volumes. The HK11 was manufactured from the early 1960s until the 1990s.

SPECIFICATION	
MANUFACTURER Heckler & Koch	
CALIBRE 7.62mm NATO	
MAGAZINE CAPACITY 20	
ACTION Gas operated	
TOTAL LENGTH 1,020mm/40.1in	
BARREL LENGTH 450mm/17.7in	
WEIGHT UNLOADED 6.7kg/14.8lb	

HK21A1

This was a development of the
CETME and Heckler & Koch G3
series, and built on much the same

belt-feed tray

stamped-steel receiver as the G3 rifle. Firing from the same delayed roller lock as
other Heckler & Koch weapons, the 21 has a high cyclic rate for a Light Machine
Gun (LMG), stout recoil and brisk ejection of empties. Based on the G3
receiver, it is too light to be a real General-Purpose Machine Gun (GPMG).
The A1 had the optional box magazine feed (and attendant parts) eliminated
from the standard 21. The HK21A1 was in use from the early 1960s to the 1990s.

SPECIFICATION	
MANUFACTURER Heckler & Koch	
CALIBRE 7.62mm NATO, 7.62 x 39mm, 5.56 x 45mm	
MAGAZINE CAPACITY Belt-fed	
ACTION Recoil operated/roller-lock delay	
TOTAL LENGTH 1,018mm/40.1in	
BARREL LENGTH 575mm/22.63in	
WEIGHT UNLOADED 6.66kg/14.7lb	

MG 14/17

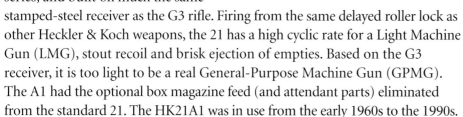

Also known as a "Zeppelin gun", the MG 14 derived
from a need for automatic weapons for the Imperial Air Corps. The designers
took a Maxim, lightened it to the extreme, took off the water jacket and turned
the toggle lock upside down. By the end of World War I, the need for
automatic weapons was so great that the MG 14 was fitted with a buttstock,
bipod and forward handgrip. The resulting MG 14/17 was then handed to the
infantry for use as a ground weapon and was not too heavy in the infantry role.
It was in use from 1914 to 1918, obsolete at the end of the war and mostly
confiscated in war reparations.

SPECIFICATION	
MANUFACTURER Mauser	
CALIBRE 7.92 x 57mm	
MAGAZINE CAPACITY Belt-fed	
ACTION Recoil operated/toggle lock	
TOTAL LENGTH 1,422mm/56in	
BARREL LENGTH 717mm/28.25in	
WEIGHT UNLOADED 11kg/24.25lb	

MG 34

With Versailles
prohibiting new

dual trigger for full
and semi fire

Maxims, Germany turned to Mauser who developed the first General-Purpose
Machine Gun. It had a quick-change barrel, it was selective fire and used a belt
or two different-sized drums, all in a lightweight package. It was not just light by
World War I Maxim standards; the weight would be acceptable today.
Ultimately it proved too well made and not loose enough for the mud of
combat. It also took too much time to manufacture, requiring many precise
machining operations. It was in use in Germany from 1934 to 1945.

SPECIFICATION	
MANUFACTURER Mauser	
CALIBRE 7.92 x 57mm	
MAGAZINE CAPACITY Belt, 50- and 75-round drums	
ACTION Recoil operated/roller locked	
TOTAL LENGTH 1,220mm/48in	
BARREL LENGTH 623mm/24.6in	
WEIGHT UNLOADED 12.02kg/26.5lb	

MG 42/59

recoil booster

SPECIFICATION

MANUFACTURER Rheinmettal

CALIBRE 7.92 x 57mm

MAGAZINE CAPACITY Belt-fed

ACTION Recoil operated

TOTAL LENGTH 1,220mm/48in

BARREL LENGTH 533mm/21in

WEIGHT UNLOADED 11.56kg/25.5lb

The first machine guns produced after the end of World War II, issued to the Border Police, were simply MG42s built on wartime machinery and still chambered in 7.92mm. During the 1950s the design was modified and the calibre changed to eventually become the MG 3. The changes gradually brought down the cyclic rate (as much as 1,300 rpm in the MG 42) and increased durability. It was produced from 1948 to the late 1960s and called the MG42/59.

Dreyse MG 13

SPECIFICATION

MANUFACTURER RM&M

CALIBRE 7.92 x 57mm

MAGAZINE CAPACITY Drum, 25, 7, 50 round

ACTION Recoil operated

TOTAL LENGTH 1,220mm/48in

BARREL LENGTH 717mm/28.25in

WEIGHT UNLOADED 10.89kg/24.0lb

This was a rebuilt Dreyse machine gun, converted for use as a "light" infantry weapon. With a perforated air-cooling jacket, bipod and saddle drum, it was quickly made obsolete by the MG 34. It was soon sold off to Portugal, where it was known as the M38. The Dreyse MG 13 was not at all common and only in service only from 1930 until 1939.

MG 08/15

drum for belted ammo

SPECIFICATION

MANUFACTURER Various

CALIBRE 7.92 x 57mm

MAGAZINE CAPACITY Belt, 50-round drum

ACTION Recoil operated/toggle lock

TOTAL LENGTH 1,435mm/56.5in

BARREL LENGTH 716mm/28.2in

WEIGHT UNLOADED 17.7kg/39lb without
water

The Maxim MG 08 was a nearly indestructible engine of death in the trench warfare of World War I. What it was not, however, was portable. The MG 08/15 had the sledge removed, a bipod and butt stock affixed and a sling attached. The water jacket was left on, but it was a dull infantryman who failed to drain the water before exiting the trenches on an assault. Even with the reduction in weight, trying to wrestle it across a shell-churned battlefield had to be back-breaking. Still, anything that increased mobility was an improvement. It was used only in World War I from 1915 to 1918. Some were found in World War II in guard towers at armouries and death camps.

MG 42

SPECIFICATION

MANUFACTURER Various

CALIBRE 7.92 x 57mm

MAGAZINE CAPACITY Belt-fed

ACTION Recoil operated/roller locked

TOTAL LENGTH 1,220mm/48in

BARREL LENGTH 533mm/21in

WEIGHT UNLOADED 11.56kg/25.5lb

The MG 42 was made primarily of steel stampings and did away with the excesses of design of the MG 34: the 42 fed only from the left side, it was not select-fire, and it had no provision for magazine feed. It used a roller-lock, with a gas boost to the mechanism gained from the adjustable muzzle cone. The cyclic rate was 1,200 to 1,300 rpm, but the quick-change barrel was so easy to change that heating hardly mattered. It was produced in huge volumes from 1942 to 1945 and again after the war both for West Germany and for export.

Italy

Italy entered World War I with a motley collection of machine guns. Forces had to contend with machine guns made in two different locally produced rifle calibres (6.5 and 7.35mm) and a large supply of 8 x 50R Schwarzlose guns that were war reparations from Austria. Mussolini's emphasis on production did not help, as much effort went to political favourites instead of a few standard and debugged designs.

Breda M30

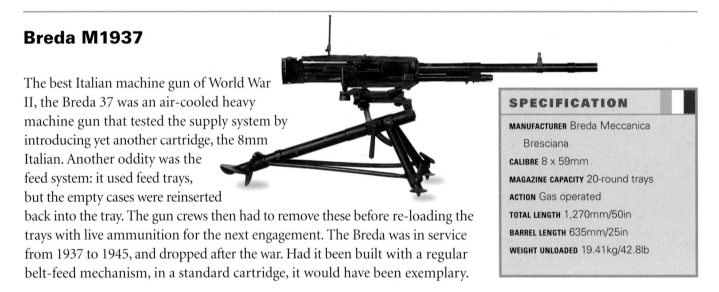

magazine on right side

A re-introduction of the Breda 1924, the M30 featured an Italian novelty: a permanently attached magazine which fed from the right, and was hinged to open when the gunner pushed it forward. He would recharge an empty magazine by means of a special charger with 20 rounds in it. The delayed blowback system produced a rather violent primary extraction, so the cases had to be oiled as they were fed, via a built-in cartridge oiler. These issues did not discourage the Italian Army from buying many M30s. Breda even exported some in 7 and 7.92mm Mauser. They were in service from 1930 to 1945.

SPECIFICATION

MANUFACTURER Breda
CALIBRE 6.5 x 52mm
MAGAZINE CAPACITY 20
ACTION Delayed blowback
TOTAL LENGTH 1232mm/48.50in
BARREL LENGTH 520mm/20.50in
WEIGHT UNLOADED 10.31kg/22.75lb w/o mount

Breda M1937

The best Italian machine gun of World War II, the Breda 37 was an air-cooled heavy machine gun that tested the supply system by introducing yet another cartridge, the 8mm Italian. Another oddity was the feed system: it used feed trays, but the empty cases were reinserted back into the tray. The gun crews then had to remove these before re-loading the trays with live ammunition for the next engagement. The Breda was in service from 1937 to 1945, and dropped after the war. Had it been built with a regular belt-feed mechanism, in a standard cartridge, it would have been exemplary.

SPECIFICATION

MANUFACTURER Breda Meccanica Bresciana
CALIBRE 8 x 59mm
MAGAZINE CAPACITY 20-round trays
ACTION Gas operated
TOTAL LENGTH 1,270mm/50in
BARREL LENGTH 635mm/25in
WEIGHT UNLOADED 19.41kg/42.8lb

Colt 1914

The 1914 was simply the Colt 1895 chambered in 6.5 Carcano, and manufactured in the early years of World War I. As an air-cooled machine gun it was prone to over-heating in the sustained fire of World War I tactical use. However, the medium-power 6.5 cartridge was a lesser heat source for the barrel, and the Italian guns were probably less prone to overheating than the more powerful .30-06 of the American versions. Despite the success of the Colt, they were not retained after the war, and were replaced by a steady succession of Italian designs of dubious reliability. They were in service during Italy's involvement in World War I, from 1915 to 1918.

SPECIFICATION

MANUFACTURER Colt
CALIBRE 6.5 x 52mm
MAGAZINE CAPACITY Belt-fed
ACTION Gas operated
TOTAL LENGTH 1,036mm/40.80in
BARREL LENGTH 711mm/28.0in
WEIGHT UNLOADED 18.14kg/40lb w/o mount

FIAT-Revelli 1914

As water-cooled heavy machine guns of the World War I period go, the Revelli was relatively lightweight. Chambered in the Italian 6.5mm cartridge, it should have been a steady performer, but any delayed blowback action had the potential to be unreliable with any ammunition that was not perfect. The bolt was not completely enclosed by the receiver, so it would cycle out of the rear, directly toward the firer. Also, the feed mechanism was a bottleneck in any sustained-fire situation. Instead of a belt, the Revelli used a sheet-metal contraption called a cage, holding 50 rounds in ten columns of five. The block of exposed cartridges was inserted into the left side. It would feed each column to the chamber, and then eject the empty feed cage out. The cages were not robust enough to survive many firings. The ammunition manufacturer would have to provide a new feed cage for each 50-round ammunition increment. It is hard to imagine why the designers thought the cage an improvement on a belt-fed system. Desperate for machine guns, the Italians bought the Revelli. After the war, they were put into storage and not seen again.

ammunition cage

SPECIFICATION

MANUFACTURER FIAT-Revelli
CALIBRE 6.5 x 52mm
MAGAZINE CAPACITY 50
ACTION Delayed blowback
TOTAL LENGTH 1,181mm/46.5in
BARREL LENGTH 654mm/25.75in
WEIGHT UNLOADED 17kg/37.5lb (no water)

FIAT M35

breechblock

SPECIFICATION

MANUFACTURER FIAT-Revelli
CALIBRE 8 x 59mm
MAGAZINE CAPACITY Belt-fed
ACTION Delayed blowback
TOTAL LENGTH 1270mm/50in
BARREL LENGTH 654mm/25.75in
WEIGHT UNLOADED 22.6kg/50lb

The Revelli 1914 was quite dated by 1935, so FIAT was asked to update its machine gun. It did so by changing from a water-cooled to an air-cooled barrel. It also increased the calibre, but kept the same delayed blowback action. The result was yet another machine gun that required lubricated cartridges to avoid broken cases and another seized-up machine gun in combat. Additionally, the 8mm cartridge further taxed the Italian production and supply system, which could only be charitably described as disorganized. It was in service only from 1935 to 1945, and immediately scrapped when the war was over.

Vickers Class C

SPECIFICATION

MANUFACTURER Vickers
CALIBRE 6.5 x 52mm
MAGAZINE CAPACITY Belt-fed
ACTION Recoil operated
TOTAL LENGTH 1,100mm/43.3in
BARREL LENGTH 720mm/28.34in
WEIGHT UNLOADED 33kg/72.75lb
(no water)

This was the export C model of the Vickers Company, shipped to Italy before and during World War I. The 6.5mm Carcano round would have made for a quiet, low-recoiling and slow-to-heat-up heavy machine gun. Italy would have done well to have simply retained the Vickers in 6.5mm, rather than try other designs such as the later short adoption of the 7.35mm cartridge. But had they stuck with it, their Vickers could have been converted for far less effort than designing and manufacturing a whole new machine gun. It was in service from 1910 to 1918.

Norway

When Norway separated from Sweden in 1905, it went to Denmark and the United States for machine guns: both countries were established and reliable performers. Between the wars, the choice of established machine guns to purchase was limited.

It was not that there were many contenders: the list of reliable machine guns was short and Norway was ill-equipped. The Danish Madsen was the standard machine gun and reasonably effective. The Browning MG M29 could be unreliable in cold weather.

Browning MG M29

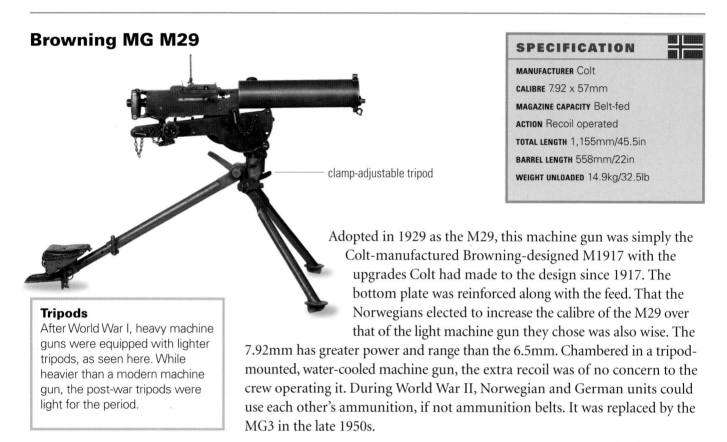

clamp-adjustable tripod

SPECIFICATION	
MANUFACTURER Colt	
CALIBRE 7.92 x 57mm	
MAGAZINE CAPACITY Belt-fed	
ACTION Recoil operated	
TOTAL LENGTH 1,155mm/45.5in	
BARREL LENGTH 558mm/22in	
WEIGHT UNLOADED 14.9kg/32.5lb	

Tripods
After World War I, heavy machine guns were equipped with lighter tripods, as seen here. While heavier than a modern machine gun, the post-war tripods were light for the period.

Adopted in 1929 as the M29, this machine gun was simply the Colt-manufactured Browning-designed M1917 with the upgrades Colt had made to the design since 1917. The bottom plate was reinforced along with the feed. That the Norwegians elected to increase the calibre of the M29 over that of the light machine gun they chose was also wise. The 7.92mm has greater power and range than the 6.5mm. Chambered in a tripod-mounted, water-cooled machine gun, the extra recoil was of no concern to the crew operating it. During World War II, Norwegian and German units could use each other's ammunition, if not ammunition belts. It was replaced by the MG3 in the late 1950s.

Madsen M1922

While Norway offered many locations where a heavy machine gun could do great damage to an attacker, after World War I, all armies realized the need for a portable machine gun. Norway selected the Madsen. Despite the extra cost of manufacture and procurement, and the odd operating system, the Madsen was a proven reliable performer. Chambered in 6.5mm, the Madsen could use rifle ammunition. That the 6.5mm has mild recoil is also an advantage to the operator, allowing for more-accurate fire. Adopted in the mid-1920s, the Madsen was obviously obsolete after World War II and not replaced. Along with the Browning, it was replaced by the MG3, a General-Purpose Machine Gun (GPMG) that could perform well in both roles.

ABOVE The cocking lever on the side betrays the Madsen's age.

SPECIFICATION	
MANUFACTURER Kongsberg Våpenfabrikk	
CALIBRE 6.5 x 55mm	
MAGAZINE CAPACITY 20, 25 & 30	
ACTION Recoil operated	
TOTAL LENGTH 1,168mm/46in	
BARREL LENGTH 482mm/19in	
WEIGHT UNLOADED 9.97kg/22lb	

 Denmark

A peninsula in the Baltic, Denmark has a long history of fending off its neighbours, not always with success. Despite little in the way of natural resources, Denmark built a solid firearms production base. After World War II, Denmark left the arms-making field, in the face of increased competition from larger countries.

Madsen M1946

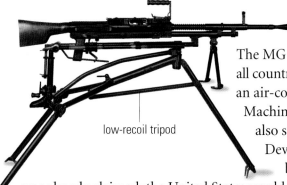

SPECIFICATION

MANUFACTURER Dansk Industri Syndikat

CALIBRE 7.62 x 63mm

MAGAZINE CAPACITY 20, 25, 30 & 40-round magazines (.30-06 were 30-round)

ACTION Recoil operated

TOTAL LENGTH 1,168mm/46in

BARREL LENGTH 482mm/19in

WEIGHT UNLOADED 9.97kg/22lb

The Madsen light machine gun was distributed widely from 1902. Although awkward in appearance it was easy to handle. The long-recoil design made for brisk, but manageable recoil. Relatively expensive to manufacture, and requiring good-quality ammunition, it worked well when treated well. That, combined with its relative light weight, made it popular around the world. Offered in a host of calibres, the M1946 was made in .30-06 for Denmark. Since it was using the American M1 Garand at the time, keeping the calibre supply simple was wise. It was used from 1946 until Denmark switched to the 7.62mm with the rest of Europe and was replaced by the Madsen-Saetter.

Madsen-Saetter

low-recoil tripod

SPECIFICATION

MANUFACTURER Dansk Industri Syndikat

CALIBRE 7.62 x 51mm

MAGAZINE CAPACITY 50, 7, 100-round magazines, and belts

ACTION Gas operated/rotating bolt

TOTAL LENGTH 1,219mm/48in

BARREL LENGTH 660mm/26in

WEIGHT UNLOADED 11.61kg/25.6lb

The MG 42 had shown the way, and all countries after World War II wanted an air-cooled General-Purpose Machine Gun (GPMG), that could also serve in the support role. Development took until 1959, by which time the market was already claimed: the United States would make their own, the Soviets would make them for any client state, and FN would sell MAG 58s to the rest of the world. The Madsen-Saetter could be manufactured in any rimless cartridge from 6.5mm to 7.92mm. It fed from either belts or box magazines, unusual for this type of gun. The Madsen-Saetter was never a commercial success and it saw only limited production beginning in 1959.

SPECIFICATION

MANUFACTURER Vickers

CALIBRE 8 x 58R

MAGAZINE CAPACITY Belt-fed

ACTION Gas operated/toggle

TOTAL LENGTH 1,092mm/43in

BARREL LENGTH 721mm/28.4in

WEIGHT UNLOADED 14.96kg/33lb

Vickers Commercial C Model

As good as the Madsen machine gun proved to be, it was not a heavy, support-role machine gun. The only way to accomplish that, before World War II, was with a water-cooled machine gun. Thus, Denmark acquired a supply of Vickers heavy machine guns in the early 1920s. They were chambered in the Danish rifle calibre, 8 x 58R, a simple change for the Vickers Company to have made. Nearly all of them ended up being appropriated to feed the German war machine after the German occupation of Denmark.

SAV Model 40

curved gas tubes

This was an odd light machine gun, built by the Swedes and used by some Waffen-SS units as the MG 35/36. The distinctive loops of the gas system made it easy to identify. It was unpopular with every unit it was issued to. Eventually it was withdrawn from regular Swedish service and sent to the Home Guard units, who also hated it. It was replaced after a short service life between 1940 and 1945 by the M1921 Browning.

SPECIFICATION	
MANUFACTURER SAV	
CALIBRE 6.5 x 55mm	
MAGAZINE CAPACITY 20	
ACTION Gas operated	
TOTAL LENGTH 1,257mm/49.48in	
BARREL LENGTH 685mm/26.96in	
WEIGHT UNLOADED 8.5kg/18.73lb	

Czech Republic

After World War I, the Austro-Hungarian Empire was divided into countries of similar ethnic backgrounds, with the Czechs and Slovaks amalgamated into a new country known as Czechoslovakia. After World War II, the country was a Warsaw Pact ally. With the fall of the Soviet Union, the two groups went their separate ways. With many natural resources and a manufacturing history, it is little wonder Czech designs are common.

VZ26

finned barrel for greater air-cooling

One of the first light machine guns, now called a Squad Automatic Weapon (SAW), the VZ26 (also ZB26) was popular enough to be made on three continents and used by two dozen countries. As a milled-receiver magazine-fed weapon, it was relatively easy to produce in any cartridge that fitted the basic receiver/bolt dimensions. When built on contract, it could be delivered in a variety of chambering choices. It was quickly improved and upgraded. The VZ26 was the design and tactical forerunner to the BREN gun. Production began in 1926 and it was used until the late 1940s.

SPECIFICATION	
MANUFACTURER CZ BRio	
CALIBRE 7.92 x 57mm, 6.5mm Jap	
MAGAZINE CAPACITY 20	
ACTION Gas operated/tilting bolt	
TOTAL LENGTH 1,163mm/45.8in	
BARREL LENGTH 602mm/23.7in	
WEIGHT UNLOADED 9.65kg/21.28lb	

VZ37

dual pistol grips/handles

The forerunner to the British BESA machine gun, the VZ37 (also ZB37) was a heavy machine gun meant to be used from a tripod. The barrel moved fore and aft and the cartridge was chambered and fired during forward movement. The recoil of firing had to thus overcome the forward inertia of the barrel. It was compact for a heavy machine gun and used a pair of side-grasping/firing handles that were pitched downwards. The Czechs manufactured them from 1937 until Germany invaded, and then for the Germans until 1945. After the war, there were many other designs found in greater numbers, so production ceased.

SPECIFICATION	
MANUFACTURER CZ BRio	
CALIBRE 7.92 x 57mm	
MAGAZINE CAPACITY Belt-fed	
ACTION Gas operated	
TOTAL LENGTH 1,105mm/43.5in	
BARREL LENGTH 678mm/26.7in	
WEIGHT UNLOADED 18.96kg/41.8lb	

Kalas

SPEC

MANUFACT

CALIBRE 7.

MAGAZINE

ACTION Ga

TOTAL LEN

BARREL LE

WEIGHT UI

16.5-

Chau

SPE

MANUFA

CALIBRE

MAGAZI

ACTION

TOTAL L

BARREL

WEIGHT

Sout
on th
Sout

Ve

VZ60

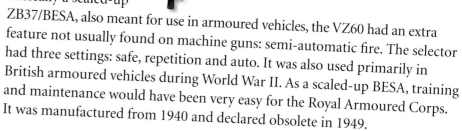

SPECIFICATION

MANUFACTURER CZ BRio

CALIBRE 15mm

MAGAZINE CAPACITY 25-round belt

ACTION Gas operated

TOTAL LENGTH 2,050mm/80.75in

BARREL LENGTH 640mm/25.2in

WEIGHT UNLOADED 56.9kg/125.5lb

Basically a scaled-up ZB37/BESA, also meant for use in armoured vehicles, the VZ60 had an extra feature not usually found on machine guns: semi-automatic fire. The selector had three settings: safe, repetition and auto. It was also used primarily in British armoured vehicles during World War II. As a scaled-up BESA, training and maintenance would have been very easy for the Royal Armoured Corps. It was manufactured from 1940 and declared obsolete in 1949.

VZ52/57

SPECIFICATION

MANUFACTURER CZ BRio

CALIBRE 7.62 x 39mm

MAGAZINE CAPACITY 25-round box,
100-round belt

ACTION Gas operated/tilting bolt

TOTAL LENGTH 1,041mm/41in

BARREL LENGTH 541mm/21.3in

WEIGHT UNLOADED 7.98kg/17.6lb

A new and improved post-war ZB26/30 or BREN gun, the VZ52 was designed to be fed from a belt or box magazine. Complex and sophisticated, it pre-dated the current SAWs such as the M249 or Minimi that also fed from either box or belt. As a bonus, it featured a quick-change barrel. The VZ52 was chambered in the new Czech intermediate cartridge, the 7.62 x 45mm. The 52/57 was the designation given to the original light machine gun rebuilt to use the Soviet M43 cartridge, the 7.62 x 39mm. The Czechs began making it in 1952 and, after the calibre change, continued to manufacture it into the late 1960s.

UK 59

SPECIFICATION

MANUFACTURER CZ BRio

CALIBRE 7.62 x 54R

MAGAZINE CAPACITY Belt-fed

ACTION Gas operated/tilting bolt

TOTAL LENGTH 1,217mm/47.9in

BARREL LENGTH 693mm/27.3in

WEIGHT UNLOADED 19.23kg/42.4lb
w/heavy barrel, on tripod.
8.66kg/19.1lb in bipod

This was the Czech answer to the desire for a General-Purpose Machine Gun (GPMG) that could be used on a bipod for squad use and on a tripod for support fire. The feed mechanism is basically that of the ZB37 combined with the quick-change barrel design of the ZB52. Chambered for the Soviet rimmed .30, the 7.62 x 54R, it was manufactured from machined forgings, and was thus somewhat heavy and expensive to manufacture. While production was still underway, it was altered slightly (and the name changed to UK68) when re-chambered for 7.62mm NATO. It is in current use with both the Czech and Slovak armies.

Schwarzlose VZ7/24

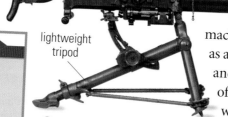

lightweight
tripod

SPECIFICATION

MANUFACTURER Steyr

CALIBRE 7.92 x 57mm

MAGAZINE CAPACITY Belt-fed

ACTION Blowback

TOTAL LENGTH 1,066mm/42in

BARREL LENGTH 527mm/20.75in

WEIGHT UNLOADED 19.95kg/44lb

The Schwarzlose is perhaps unique in belt-fed rifle-calibre machine guns in not having a locked breech. Known as a blowback action, the design needs a heavy bolt and/or a stout recoil spring to contain the power of the cartridge and to prevent battering and quick weapon demise. The Schwarzlose has both. Germany used Schwarzlose machine guns in World War I and World War II, the latter chambered in the standard 7.92mm cartridge. The M07/24 was common enough to have specialized equipment such as belt loaders and training manuals printed for use by Wehrmacht troops in World War I. Production began in 1907. It was rebuilt as the VZ7/24 in 1924, and used in German service until 1945.

Vector Mini SS

The Mini SS is the SS77 receiver built in 5.56mm calibre. The Mini SS is also found as a parts or conversion kit, containing all the parts needed to rebuild a 7.62mm SS77 that uses 5.56mm ammunition. As a result it is only a bit lighter but cannot be less durable than the larger calibre general-purpose machine gun (GPMG). While 8.26kg/18.21lb is fairly heavy for a squad automatic weapon (SAW), which is what most 5.56mm machine guns are, the durability of such an approach cannot be faulted. Conversions began in 1994 and the Mini SS is presently in use.

SPECIFICATION	
MANUFACTURER Lyttelton	
CALIBRE 5.56 x 45mm	
MAGAZINE CAPACITY Belt-fed	
ACTION Gas operated	
TOTAL LENGTH 1,000mm/39.37in	
BARREL LENGTH 515mm/20.27in	
WEIGHT UNLOADED 8.26kg/18.21lb	

Vickers conversions

Not only were the Vickers rebuilt to 7.62mm by the South African forces, the weapons were updated to the new calibre in the 1960s and served for several decades. The conversions required new barrels, altering the feed system for the shorter cartridge, and exchanging action springs. The Vickers would be fine for vehicular or fortification use, but it was by no means a portable weapon in the modern sense. Once a replacement was named, the machine guns were dismantled and the parts were sold as surplus.

SPECIFICATION	
MANUFACTURER Vickers	
CALIBRE 7.62 x 51mm	
MAGAZINE CAPACITY Belt-fed	
ACTION Recoil operated	
TOTAL LENGTH 1,158mm/45.6in	
BARREL LENGTH 724mm/28.5in	
WEIGHT UNLOADED 14.96kg/33lb	

Serbia

As Yugoslavia, prior to the dissolution into five independent countries in the 1990s, this region produced many small arms for use by other Warsaw-Pact or communist-aligned countries. It also went further with the Kalashnikov design, chambering it in calibres not found in the Soviet Union.

Maxim MG08

As part of the Austro-Hungarian Empire before and during World War I, it would be natural to find Maxim machine guns in Yugoslavia. Except for the markings required by Yugoslavian purchase, they would not have varied from German-issue heavy machine guns of the period. They also would have been turned against the army of their former manufacturers when Germany invaded Yugoslavia in 1941. The Maxim MG08 was in service from 1908 to 1945.

ABOVE The Maxim has more than just an ejection port because a lengthy cloth belt had to be expelled. The exit tray is to control the belt to keep it from catching in the ejection port.

SPECIFICATION	
MANUFACTURER Spandau	
CALIBRE 7.92 x 57mm	
MAGAZINE CAPACITY Belt-fed	
ACTION Recoil operated	
TOTAL LENGTH 1,175mm/46.25in	
BARREL LENGTH 717mm/28.25in	
WEIGHT UNLOADED 18.37kg/40.5lb	
w/o water or mount	

Sarac M53

SPECIFICATION	
MANUFACTURER Zastava	
CALIBRE 7.92 x 57mm	
MAGAZINE CAPACITY Belt-fed	
ACTION Recoil operated	
TOTAL LENGTH 1,219mm/48in	
BARREL LENGTH 533mm/21in	
WEIGHT UNLOADED 11.56kg/25.5lb	

This was the MG 42, built in Yugoslavia, and offered for export. While the 7.62 x 51mm version would be expected to work faultlessly, the proposed but never-seen .30-06 version probably would have had problems. It did not matter, as there were plenty of buyers and lots of ammunition available for the 7.92 x 57mm version. Buyers who were locked into the 7.62 x 51mm cartridge would find the Sarac altogether reliable. Manufacture of the M53 began in 1953 and continued until the dissolution of Yugoslavia in the 1990s.

M72 Kalashnikov

SPECIFICATION	
MANUFACTURER Zastava	
CALIBRE 7.62 x 39mm	
MAGAZINE CAPACITY 30, 40	
ACTION Gas operated	
TOTAL LENGTH 1,040mm/40.94in	
BARREL LENGTH 591mm/23.26in	
WEIGHT UNLOADED 5kg/11.02lb	

longer barrel than AK

Interchangeable parts
All parts of the RKP can be used with the AK or AKM, making the unit armourer's job easier.

This is simply the Yugoslavian RPK, in the standard Soviet chambering. The Yugoslavian manufacturing and design process of the M72 created a distinctive bulge in the receiver, caused by the bulged trunnion inside (the steel block securing the barrel and receiver). The longer barrel added little muzzle velocity but did add a significant sighting radius. The bipod was necessary, as the M72 (and other RPKs) were commonly issued with 40-round magazines. The bipod kept the magazine off the ground, although it also made the firer a slightly taller target. It was manufactured from the 1960s to the 1980s.

M84 PKM

stock specific to the M84

SPECIFICATION	
MANUFACTURER Zastava	
CALIBRE 7.62 x 54R	
MAGAZINE CAPACITY Belt-fed	
ACTION Gas operated	
TOTAL LENGTH 1,173mm/46.18in	
BARREL LENGTH 658mm/25.90in	
WEIGHT UNLOADED 8.99kg/19.81lb	

Modern Kalashnikov
PKM means "Machine-gun Kalashnikov Modernized".

The M84 was a clone of the Soviet PKM with very few differences. While the Soviet Union exported firearms at times for ideological reasons, the Yugoslavians did so only for cash. The Yugoslavian M84, like all PKMs, fired from an open bolt, and the cartridges must (the rims dictate it) be extracted rearwards from the belt on each firing cycle, before then being fed forward into the chamber. It was manufactured from the early 1960s to the 1990s.

Hungary

Prior to World War I, Hungary was a province of the Austro-Hungarian empire, and as such used the arms the Empire required. After World War I, with a communist revolution suppressed and territory lost, Hungary slowly allied itself with Germany. When Germany invaded the Soviet Union, Hungary became a full Axis ally. As with all countries occupied by the Soviet Union after World War I, Hungary adopted the Soviet pattern machine guns. They were manufactured at FÉG, the national arms factory.

PKM

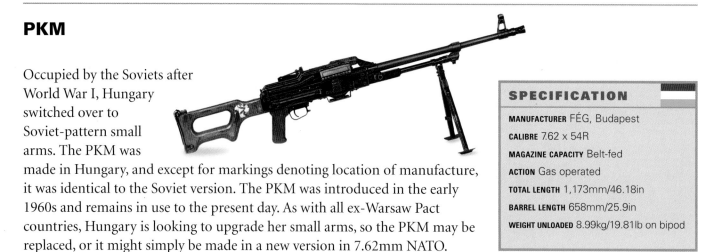

Occupied by the Soviets after World War I, Hungary switched over to Soviet-pattern small arms. The PKM was made in Hungary, and except for markings denoting location of manufacture, it was identical to the Soviet version. The PKM was introduced in the early 1960s and remains in use to the present day. As with all ex-Warsaw Pact countries, Hungary is looking to upgrade her small arms, so the PKM may be replaced, or it might simply be made in a new version in 7.62mm NATO.

SPECIFICATION

MANUFACTURER FÉG, Budapest
CALIBRE 7.62 x 54R
MAGAZINE CAPACITY Belt-fed
ACTION Gas operated
TOTAL LENGTH 1,173mm/46.18in
BARREL LENGTH 658mm/25.9in
WEIGHT UNLOADED 8.99kg/19.81lb on bipod

Goryunov

shoulder stock added for use at squad level

The medium machine gun of the Soviet Union during Word War II, it was adopted by Hungary after the war. It was replaced by the PKM as supplies became available. It was in service only from 1945 until the mid 1960s.

SPECIFICATION

MANUFACTURER FÉG, Budapest
CALIBRE 7.62 x 54R
MAGAZINE CAPACITY Belt-fed
ACTION Gas operated
TOTAL LENGTH 1,150mm/45.27in
BARREL LENGTH 720mm/28.3in
WEIGHT UNLOADED 13.8kg/30.41lb (gun only, not carriage or shield)

Solothurn M31M

dual triggers for full and semi-fire

Denied possession of heavy machine guns by the Treaty of Versailles, Germany investigated light machine guns. Designed by Louis Schmeisser at Rheinmettal, the Solothurn M31M was rejected by the German Army, but produced in Switzerland and Austria for export. It was in use in Hungary from 1930 until 1945. Although the Hungarian Army served alongside German units on the Eastern Front and was often directed by German commanders, it retained its own small arms and calibre.

SPECIFICATION

MANUFACTURER Steyr-Daimler-Puch AG
CALIBRE 8 x 56R
MAGAZINE CAPACITY 30
ACTION Short recoil
TOTAL LENGTH 1,170mm/46.06in
BARREL LENGTH 600mm/23.6in
WEIGHT UNLOADED 9.5kg/20.93lb

 # Greece

After separating from Turkey, Greece re-armed with "modern" small arms when it would have done well to retain the German small arms that Turkey had used.

Between the wars, Greece tried to remain neutral to ensure her security. When World War II broke out and this was no longer possible, Greece sided with the Allies.

Hotchkiss M1926

rear monopod for long-range fire

SPECIFICATION	
MANUFACTURER	St Etienne
CALIBRE	6.5 x 54mm
MAGAZINE CAPACITY	Belt-fed
ACTION	Gas operated
TOTAL LENGTH	1,180mm/45.5in
BARREL LENGTH	597mm/23.5in
WEIGHT UNLOADED	9.97kg/22lb

The Hotchkiss firm did not stop between the wars, and developed light machine guns for export. The Model 1926 for Greece was a belt-fed light machine gun that was greatly refined from the 1909 Portative. Hotchkiss could not find other export markets for such a well-made light machine gun due to the intense competition within the arms market between the wars. That competition, combined with the huge volume of surplus arms, made it a difficult time to make a living selling machine guns. They were only in service until World War II – after the war, Greece converted to American small arms and ammunition.

 # Finland

Bristly about the independence it painfully acquired in 1917-1918, Finland has struggled to remain free of Russian control since. It sided with the Germans against the Soviets in World War II at its cost. To protect its arms production capacity, it supplied maps without firearm-producing towns for decades.

Maxim M09/21

rear sight folded

M-21 tripod, lighter in weight

SPECIFICATION	
MANUFACTURER	Tula, Russia
CALIBRE	7.62 x 54R
MAGAZINE CAPACITY	Belt-fed
ACTION	Recoil operated/toggle lock
TOTAL LENGTH	1,110mm/43.7in
BARREL LENGTH	720mm/28.3in
WEIGHT UNLOADED	24.0kg/52.9lb (tripod adds 27.6kg/60.8lb)

This was one of three heavy machine guns, all Maxims, used by Finland. The 21 part of the model designation refers to the tripod. All Finnish heavy machine guns were Maxims, wrested from Russia or captured from armouries during Finland's break from the Russians. The M09/09 used the original wheeled mount whereas the 09/21 model used a tripod modelled after a pre-World War I Maxim tripod design, saving over 8kg/17.6lb from the 09/09 weight. From independence in 1918 to weapons retirement or upgrades in 1945, the Finnish Maxim could be counted on to keep Finnish borders intact.

Russian-based arms
It was not only logical that Finland's smaller army would use Russian-based small arms, it was also predictable that high-quality manufacturing standards would have been sought.

Valmet M-60 type B

Where it differs from the AK-47, the Valmet M-60 improves on it. The handguards are sturdier and actually protect the hands from heat (the AK and AKM hand-guards can get quite hot in sustained firing.) The rear sight is on the receiver cover, for better accuracy. The stock is a steel tube, stronger than the laminated wood of the AK. As an early rifle or Squad Automatic Weapon (SAW), it was a better rifle. Production began in 1960 and samples are still in use to the present day.

SPECIFICATION

MANUFACTURER	Valmet
CALIBRE	7.62 x 39mm
MAGAZINE CAPACITY	30
ACTION	Gas operated/rotating bolt
TOTAL LENGTH	914mm/35.9in
BARREL LENGTH	420mm/16.5in
WEIGHT UNLOADED	4.3kg/9.47lb

Lahti M39/44

muzzle brake

At the start of World War II,
20mm anti-tank weapons were considered ineffective
against all but the lightest tanks. The M39 was, however, a relatively portable weapon that the Finns put to good use besides shooting armoured vehicles. The 20mm explosive projectile did well on bunkers and the vehicles of supply convoys. The M39/44 was a full-auto variant that proved less successful in its designated role as an anti-aircraft gun: the receiver simply was not stout enough for full-auto fire. Original models were produced in 1939, the full-auto version five years later in 1944, lasting to retirement at the end of the war.

SPECIFICATION

MANUFACTURER	VKT
CALIBRE	20 x 138mm
MAGAZINE CAPACITY	10
ACTION	Gas operated/tilting lock
TOTAL LENGTH	2,240mm/88.1in
BARREL LENGTH	1300mm/51.1in
WEIGHT UNLOADED	55.9kg/123.2lb

Sampo L41

This was a prototype machine gun: an attempt to produce a weapon lighter than a Maxim, fielded at the beginning of

World War II. Only 50 were reported to be made. Some were sent to the front, for testing and to provide much-needed firepower to infantry units. At least one was captured by the Soviets, and is reported to be on display in the St Petersburg Artillery Museum. It required more work and, since existing designs worked as well, Finland used it for only a short time then dropped it from consideration.

SPECIFICATION

MANUFACTURER	VKT
CALIBRE	7.62 x 54Rmm
MAGAZINE CAPACITY	Belt-fed
ACTION	Gas operated
TOTAL LENGTH	1,180mm/46.45in
BARREL LENGTH	500mm/19.6in
WEIGHT UNLOADED	14.9kg/32.8lb

Valmet KvKK 62

This is a Finnish-designed and produced light machine gun in the Squad Automatic Weapon (SAW) role. Unfortunately it is a heavy weapon and lacks a quick-change barrel, and even as a squad weapon this limits its firepower. Barrel overheating can be a problem even in the sub-zero climate of Finland. Despite local design and manufacture, it may soon be replaced with something with more power and greater reliability (such as the PKM). The Valmet KvKK 62 was first issued in 1966 and is still in use today.

SPECIFICATION

MANUFACTURER	VKT
CALIBRE	7.62 x 39mm
MAGAZINE CAPACITY	Belt-fed
ACTION	Gas operated/tilting bolt
TOTAL LENGTH	1,080mm/42.5in
BARREL LENGTH	475mm/18.7in
WEIGHT UNLOADED	8.3kg/18.3lb

Romania

Newly independent after World War I, Romania found itself allied with Germany at the beginning of World War II. Romanian troops fought on the Eastern Front, where much of the army was destroyed at Stalingrad. When the Soviets rolled west, they invaded Romania and found a newly victorious pro-Soviet government waiting. From Austro-Hungarian Empire, to independent country, to Soviet client state in a generation, Romania had much the same rollercoaster ride that other Eastern European countries had.

PKM

SPECIFICATION

MANUFACTURER State Armoury

CALIBRE 7.62 x 54R

MAGAZINE CAPACITY Belt-fed

ACTION Gas operated

TOTAL LENGTH 1,173mm/46.18in

BARREL LENGTH 658mm/25.90in

WEIGHT UNLOADED 8.99kg/19.81lb

The standard post-war General-Purpose Machine Gun (GPMG) of the Soviet Bloc, the PKM (Pulemyot Kalashnikova Modernizirovanniy) is still in production. The PKM is the updated version of the PK. As with so many ex-Warsaw Pact countries, Romania must decide if it will change the PKM to 7.62mm NATO, leave it as it is, or replace it entirely. It has been in service from the late 1960s.

RPK

SPECIFICATION

MANUFACTURER State Armoury

CALIBRE 7.62 x 39mm

MAGAZINE CAPACITY 40 (can use standard magazines)

ACTION Gas operated/rotating bolt

TOTAL LENGTH 1,040mm/40.95in

BARREL LENGTH 591mm/23.26in

WEIGHT UNLOADED 5.0kg/11.02lb

40-round magazine

This squad automatic weapon (SAW) was nothing more than an AK with a longer barrel, strengthened receiver, altered buttstock and larger magazine. Lacking a quick-change barrel, it had limited firepower before overheating. However, as a cost-effective means of getting a bit more firepower into a squad, the RPK made some sense. It was issued from the early 1960s until the to early 1980s.

RPK74

SPECIFICATION

MANUFACTURER State Armoury

CALIBRE 5.45 x 39mm

MAGAZINE CAPACITY 45 (can use standard magazines)

ACTION Gas operated/rotating bolt

TOTAL LENGTH 1,060mm/41.73in

BARREL LENGTH 590mm/23.25in

WEIGHT UNLOADED 5.0kg/11.02lb

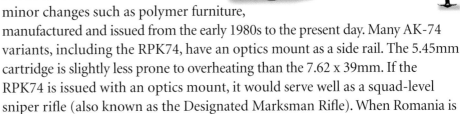

carry handle

This was the successor to the RPK with a new Soviet calibre and minor changes such as polymer furniture, manufactured and issued from the early 1980s to the present day. Many AK-74 variants, including the RPK74, have an optics mount as a side rail. The 5.45mm cartridge is slightly less prone to overheating than the 7.62 x 39mm. If the RPK74 is issued with an optics mount, it would serve well as a squad-level sniper rifle (also known as the Designated Marksman Rifle). When Romania is fully a member of NATO, the AK-74s in 5.45 x 39mm will likely be withdrawn and replaced with AK-74s in 5.56 x 45mm calibre.

Bulgaria

After World War I, Bulgaria found itself with less land than previously. In the years leading to World War II, they reluctantly worked more and more with Germany. After World War II, and a member of the Warsaw Pact, they manufactured Soviet-pattern rifles. Today, the army is undergoing a series of changes.

BREN ZB39

magazine curved differently for 8 x 56R

The ZB39 (made in 1939) was a BREN variant chambered in 8 x 56R. The cartridge was the standard Austro-Hungarian service round, the ZB39 from Czechoslovakia. The combination worked quite reliably. Hungary accepted the first ZB39 light machine guns in 1939. In 1941, Germany was at Bulgaria's border, and Bulgaria reluctantly accepted Germany's aid in recovering lost territories ceded after World War I. The ZB39 was used both by Bulgarian government troops and partisans until the end of World War I. After the war, Bulgaria reluctantly became a signatory of the Warsaw Pact, and began using Soviet-pattern machine guns.

SPECIFICATION

MANUFACTURER CZ BRio
CALIBRE 8 x 56R
MAGAZINE CAPACITY 20
ACTION Gas operated
TOTAL LENGTH 1,041mm/41in
BARREL LENGTH 541mm/21.3in
WEIGHT UNLOADED 7.98kg/17.6lb

Russia

Whether Tsarist, Soviet or as a Federation, Russia has always had a big army. Keeping it supplied means either a large purchase programme, a large number of arsenals at home and occasionally both. Under the Tsars they had both, but the Soviets insisted on home production. When Germany invaded in World War II, Russia packed up the arsenals that were too close to the front and shipped them to the Urals, where production continued.

Maxim M1905

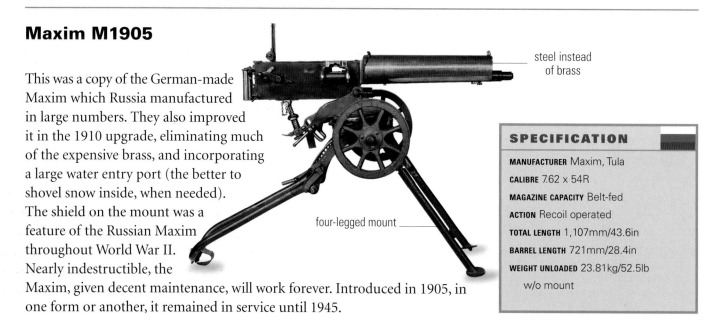

steel instead of brass

This was a copy of the German-made Maxim which Russia manufactured in large numbers. They also improved it in the 1910 upgrade, eliminating much of the expensive brass, and incorporating a large water entry port (the better to shovel snow inside, when needed). The shield on the mount was a feature of the Russian Maxim throughout World War II. Nearly indestructible, the

four-legged mount

Maxim, given decent maintenance, will work forever. Introduced in 1905, in one form or another, it remained in service until 1945.

SPECIFICATION

MANUFACTURER Maxim, Tula
CALIBRE 7.62 x 54R
MAGAZINE CAPACITY Belt-fed
ACTION Recoil operated
TOTAL LENGTH 1,107mm/43.6in
BARREL LENGTH 721mm/28.4in
WEIGHT UNLOADED 23.81kg/52.5lb
w/o mount

Lewis LMG, Russian pattern

SPECIFICATION

MANUFACTURER Savage Arms

CALIBRE 7.62 x 54R

MAGAZINE CAPACITY 47-round drum

ACTION Gas operated

TOTAL LENGTH 1,282mm/50.5in

BARREL LENGTH 668mm/26.3in

WEIGHT UNLOADED 12.33kg/27.2lb

Using a drum, the Lewis was adaptable to almost any cartridge, as long as it was not too long for the drum radius. Adapting it to the Russian cartridge was a minor matter of drum shape, bolt face and recoil springs. Despite the complexity and cost, the Lewis LMG was so well made that it proved remarkably long-lived. While the Lewis guns were made for and shipped to Tsarist Russia in 1917, they may still be in warehouses in the Russian Federation as they use the standard 7.62mm rimmed cartridge.

DP

47-round drum

SPECIFICATION

MANUFACTURER Soviet State arsenals

CALIBRE 7.62 x 54R

MAGAZINE CAPACITY 47-round drum

ACTION Gas operated

TOTAL LENGTH 1,295mm/51in

BARREL LENGTH 604mm/23.8in

WEIGHT UNLOADED 9.29kg/20.5lb

Using the firing pin to actuate the locking flaps, the DP (Degtyarev Pechotnyi) is a solid Light Machine Gun (LMG). The feed pan is a necessity due to the rimmed cartridge and the first versions had the recoil spring around the barrel. Heat could cause problems with the spring temper, it was slightly redesigned in 1943-44 to move the spring away from the heat. It was named the DPM ("M" for modernized.) In 1946, a DP built for belt-feed was unveiled, called the RP-46. This and the DP served from 1928 to the late 1950s.

SPECIFICATION

MANUFACTURER Soviet State arsenals

CALIBRE 12.7 x 108mm

MAGAZINE CAPACITY Belt-fed

ACTION Gas operated

TOTAL LENGTH 1,587mm/62.5in

BARREL LENGTH 1,069mm/42.1in

WEIGHT UNLOADED 36.28kg/80lb
w/o mount

DSHK Model 1938

This was the Soviet heavy (large calibre) machine gun in service since 1938. The cartridge is so robust that the DSHK was designed and built with a muzzle brake to reduce felt recoil, but at the cost of increased blast to the gunner. The Soviets have tried unsuccessfully to replace their heavy machine gun with an improved, lighter version for decades. The Model 1938 was the original belt-fed version with a rotary feed mechanism. It was upgraded in 1946 with a regular pawl and dogleg track feed system.

SPECIFICATION

MANUFACTURER Soviet State arsenals

CALIBRE 7.62 x 54R

MAGAZINE CAPACITY Belt-fed

ACTION Gas operated

TOTAL LENGTH 1,120mm/44.1in

BARREL LENGTH 718m/28.3in

WEIGHT UNLOADED 13.15kg/29lb
w/o mount

Goryunov SGM

The Goryunov SGM ("M" for modernized) was intended as the wartime replacement for the Maxim. It ended up not being much lighter in combat-ready condition due to the various heavy mounts it was placed on. The standard Soviet/Tsarist wheeled mount weighed 27kg/60lb without the shield, so the end result was a medium, air-cooled machine gun that did not weigh much less than the Maxim. However, the Goryunov was made in large numbers. It entered service in 1943 where it remained until the late 1950s.

PKM

Only with the arrival of the PK did the Soviets have the General-Purpose Machine Gun (GPMG) they desired. The original PK was modified to the PKM with a few mechanical changes, and a smooth barrel instead of the fluted (and thus more costly) barrel it began with. With the quick-change heavy barrel and mounted in a tripod, it can be used in support. The lighter barrel and bipod weighs only 0.5kg/1lb more than an RPD (a much less effective weapon), and is far more mobile for use by infantry units. It has been in service since 1969.

SPECIFICATION

MANUFACTURER Soviet State arsenals
CALIBRE 7.62 x 54R
MAGAZINE CAPACITY Belt-fed
ACTION Gas operated
TOTAL LENGTH 1,198mm/47.2in
BARREL LENGTH 658mm/25.9in
WEIGHT UNLOADED 7.48kg/16.5lb

RPK

Designed as a Squad Automatic Weapon (SAW), the Ruchnoi Pulemet Kalashnikova (RPK) is an AK with a stiffer receiver, longer barrel and a larger magazine. However, the AK itself overheats too quickly, so the RPK is not nearly as useful as it might first appear. As an interim weapon to supply the squad with more firepower, it was an obvious step in the mid 1950s. That it continued in service until the 1970s can only be attributed to either parsimony or extreme need. For a little more weight, the RPD is far more useful to an infantry squad. However, even the RPD overheats too quickly.

SPECIFICATION

MANUFACTURER Soviet State arsenals
CALIBRE 7.62 x 39mm
MAGAZINE CAPACITY 40 rounds
ACTION Gas operated
TOTAL LENGTH 1,039mm/40.9in
BARREL LENGTH 589mm/23.2in
WEIGHT UNLOADED 5.58kg/12.3lb

RPK-74

optical sight for squad use

This was the RPK automatic rifle translated to the AK-74 and its new 5.45mm cartridge, which does not overheat the RPK quite as quickly as the 7.62mm does. The end result is still the same: the small-unit commander has to work with an inefficient system. The RPK would be more useful if issued with optics, and used as a squad designated marksman rifle, delivering accurate semi-automatic fire at close-to-medium range. It has been in service from 1974.

SPECIFICATION

MANUFACTURER Soviet State arsenals
CALIBRE 5.45 x 39mm
MAGAZINE CAPACITY 45 rounds
ACTION Gas operated
TOTAL LENGTH 1,060mm/41.73in
BARREL LENGTH 590mm/23.22in
WEIGHT UNLOADED 5kg/11.02lb

Pecheneg

A modernized and improved PKM, the Pecheneg features forced-air cooling, a concept not used since the Lewis gun of World War I. The gas pressure of cycling the mechanism also forces air down the covering of the barrel, cooling the barrel with each shot. The designers are so sure of its function that the barrel is not one with a quick-change design built in. Only severe testing or field experience will show if the manufacturer's assertions are true. Offered as a replacement for the PKM and for export, production began in the late 1990s and continues today.

SPECIFICATION

MANUFACTURER TNTM
CALIBRE 7.62 x 54R
MAGAZINE CAPACITY Belt-fed
ACTION Gas operated
TOTAL LENGTH 1,145mm/45.07in
BARREL LENGTH 600mm/23.6in
WEIGHT UNLOADED 8.2kg/18.07lb

Egypt

Until receiving Soviet machinery, Egypt did not have an indigenous arms making capacity for machine guns and had to buy them elsewhere. The Husqvarna machinery used to make the Hakim only provided a service rifle for a short time. Since the late 1950s Egypt has been able to produce arms for itself and even export some.

Alfa

During World War II, Spain found outside sources for machine guns unavailable. Their previous suppliers were all busy making arms for the war, so they designed and produced an air-cooled heavy machine gun of their own. Initially produced in 7.92mm, the Alfa was later manufactured in 7.62mm NATO. Not surprisingly, fierce competition for post-war sales worldwide ended any chances of it being an export success. Egypt bought a few, but soon after this, they began to convert to Soviet-pattern small arms and did not need Spanish machine guns. The Alfa was produced in Spain from 1943 and used in Egypt from 1953 to 1962.

German-type low-recoil tripod

SPECIFICATION

MANUFACTURER	Alfa
CALIBRE	7.62 x 51mm
MAGAZINE CAPACITY	Belt-fed
ACTION	Gas operated
TOTAL LENGTH	1,118mm/44in
BARREL LENGTH	610mm/24in
WEIGHT UNLOADED	14.96kg/33lb

Goryunov Aswan

SPECIFICATION

MANUFACTURER	State Factory 54
CALIBRE	7.62 x 54R
MAGAZINE CAPACITY	Belt-fed
ACTION	Gas operated/side-tipping bolt
TOTAL LENGTH	1,150mm/45.27in
BARREL LENGTH	720mm/28.34in
WEIGHT UNLOADED	13.8kg/30.42lb

An air-cooled heavy machine gun built on Soviet-supplied machinery, the Aswan is simply a 1960s-era Goryunov SGM. Soviet charity had nothing to do with it; they were planning to replace the SGM with what would become the PK series and giving away tooling was simply smart politics. The Egyptians had nothing like it, so the tooling was a double blessing for them: they could both equip their army, and create jobs. The SGM is durable enough to have lasted from the early 1960s to the present day.

VZ26 copy

carry handle and quick-change handle

SPECIFICATION

MANUFACTURER	Unk
CALIBRE	7.92 x 57mm
MAGAZINE CAPACITY	20
ACTION	Gas operated/tilting bolt
TOTAL LENGTH	1,163mm/45.8in
BARREL LENGTH	602mm/23.7in
WEIGHT UNLOADED	9.65kg/21.28lb

Given the history of the area, it should come as no surprise that something as common as a VZ26 or a copy of it should be found in Egypt. Despite being a British protectorate before and during World War II, weapons could come in from all points of the compass.

 # Turkey

Despite being aligned with Germany, Turkey bought small arms from many sources, including France, where there was a large volume of surplus weapons available after World War I. The resulting mix of German and French machine guns and calibres could not have been easy on the Turkish supply system.

Hotchkiss MA4

In the 1920s, Hotchkiss developed what could have been a viable General-Purpose Machine Gun (GPMG), ten years before the German MG34. The Model 1922 (called the MA4 in Turkish service) could be manufactured to feed from a vertical box magazine, a belt or the peculiar Hotchkiss feed trays. For Turkey, Hotchkiss made it in 7.92mm calibre, but it could also be made in others. Unfortunately Hotchkiss only sold a few, mostly to Greece and Turkey. The model was scrapped after World War II.

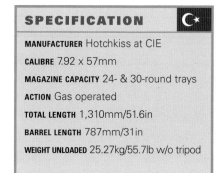

SPECIFICATION	
MANUFACTURER Hotchkiss at CIE	
CALIBRE 7.92 x 57mm	
MAGAZINE CAPACITY 24- & 30-round trays	
ACTION Gas operated	
TOTAL LENGTH 1,310mm/51.6in	
BARREL LENGTH 787mm/31in	
WEIGHT UNLOADED 25.27kg/55.7lb w/o tripod	

 # Israel

Israel had to start out with managing with whatever could be obtained from the miscellaneous collection of German and British small arms before independence. Only after establishing a sufficiently large production base could Israeli Military Industries manufacture what was both needed and desired.

Browning

built, or rebuilt to the FN two-post tripod mount

SPECIFICATION	
MANUFACTURER Colt, others	
CALIBRE 7.62mm NATO	
MAGAZINE CAPACITY Belt-fed	
ACTION Recoil operated	
TOTAL LENGTH 1,041mm/41in	
BARREL LENGTH 610mm/24in	
WEIGHT UNLOADED 14.06kg/31lb	

Tripod advantages
The benefits of a tripod are such that troops are willing to transport the extra weight. Using the control knobs on the traverse and elevation mechanism, the shooter can fire to extreme distances with accuracy, or return the gun back to a previous setting, to resume fire at a particular extreme range.

During World War II the Browning air-cooled machine gun was to be found everywhere and performed well. The basic weapon is so durable and versatile (although heavy) that it can be used in almost every role where the weight can be withstood. Inevitably, Israel converted it to 7.62mm. It was used in the War for Independence (1947–48) and can still be seen on vehicles to this day. Lighter machine guns than the Browning may be available, but few have had a longer service life.

Negev

SPECIFICATION	✡
MANUFACTURER IMI	
CALIBRE 5.56 x 45mm	
MAGAZINE CAPACITY 30, and belt-fed	
ACTION Gas operated	
TOTAL LENGTH 1,020mm/40.15in	
BARREL LENGTH 460mm/18.11in	
WEIGHT UNLOADED 7.6kg/16.75lb	

The Negev is the Israeli answer to the need for a Squad Automatic Weapon (SAW) in its modern army. The Negev looks a great deal like the FN Minimi. Like the Minimi, the Negev uses either linked belts of ammunition, or can be fed from magazines. The Negev magazine is the same as the Israeli Galil, and IMI makes adapters for the Negev allowing it to use M-16 magazines. Unlike other armies, Israel plans to replace all belt-fed machine guns with the Negev, retiring all their MAG-58s in service. Its advantages are its weight and lighter ammunition; its disadvantages are its lack of range and power. The Negev was first issued in the mid-1990s and is in use to the present day.

DROR (Johnson)

After World War II, Israel purchased the tooling for the Johnson light machine gun. Israel wanted production in-country, to avoid the problems any blockade might bring. The DROR is listed in references as having been re-designed to use .303 British ammunition. However, there are samples of the DROR in existence in .30-06, so the Israelis clearly manufactured both. As both calibres were common, and easily purchased, having weapons in both ensured Israel of being able to acquire ammunition for the Israeli Defence Force. The DROR was only in the testing phase during the battle for independence. It served from 1948 to an unknown date. The main obstacle in converting the DROR to the .303 was in accommodating the rim of the latter. It required a magazine with both a greater curvature, and a larger gap in the feed lips, than required for the American .30-06.

.30-06 ammunition used here

SPECIFICATION	✡
MANUFACTURER Johnson/Israeli	
CALIBRE .303 British,.30-06	
MAGAZINE CAPACITY 20	
ACTION Recoil operated	
TOTAL LENGTH 1,070mm/42.12in	
BARREL LENGTH 560mm/22.04in	
WEIGHT UNLOADED 10kg/22lb	

Ethiopia

A backwater in world events, Ethiopia still had to defend itself from its neighbours, and later, the aspirations of Italy under Mussolini. With no indigenous arms manufacturing, it had to import everything. That it chose the VZ30 should come as no surprise: it was the best at the time and would still be a good choice today.

VZ30

SPECIFICATION	
MANUFACTURER CZ BRio	
CALIBRE 7.92 x 57mm	
MAGAZINE CAPACITY 20	
ACTION Gas operated/tilting lock	
TOTAL LENGTH 1,163mm/45.8in	
BARREL LENGTH 602mm/23.7in	
WEIGHT UNLOADED 9.65kg/21.28lb	

An improved VZ26, the VZ30 only added to the sales and lustre of CZ and the reputation of their products. It was purchased by Ethiopia in the early 1930s, and used for decades until stocks were exhausted. Ethiopia wisely declined to design a proprietary cartridge. As the standard export light machine gun, the VZ30 in 7.92mm could be fed ammunition from any source of reliable and common 7.92 x 57mm.

Iraq

In the Cold War struggle for dominance of the Middle East and its oil, Iraq elected to go with the Soviets for small arms, military vehicles, and command and staff structure. This did not keep Saddam Hussein from accepting Western aid in the Iran-Iraq War, something Iran has not forgiven. While still purchasing weapons from non-aligned countries, the basic small arms stock was Soviet, although locally produced.

Al Quds

This was a local version of the RPD. Iraqi small arms tended to have a glossier finish than their Soviet counterparts, whether an aesthetic selection or simply a result of the steel stock selected for use is unknown. As with all belt-fed squad automatic weapons lacking a quick-change barrel, the Al Quds overheats if not used carefully. Given the extreme desert environment, over-heating and weapons maintenance was an ongoing problem for Iraqi soldiers. Also, trying to deal with Iranian MG 3s, while armed with an Al Quds in 7.62 x 39mm, had to be a real challenge. The Iraqi soldiers were out-ranged, and did not have the sustained fire capability of the MG 3. Manufacture began in the 1970s and the Al Quds can still be seen in use to the present day.

SPECIFICATION

MANUFACTURER Iraqi armouries
CALIBRE 7.62 x 39mm
MAGAZINE CAPACITY 30, 40 and 75
ACTION Gas operated
TOTAL LENGTH 1,037mm/40.8in
BARREL LENGTH 520mm/20.47in
WEIGHT UNLOADED 7.4kg/16.3lb

Magazines
The Al Quds accepts 30 and 40 magazines, but has been seen with 75-round drum magazines.

Iran/Persia

Persia was useful to Europe (and Britain) primarily as a block to Russian attempts to gain a warm-water port. However, the discovery of oil made it a much larger player on the world stage. During World War II, Iran was a transportation route for materials to the Soviets from the United States. So it did, for a brief time, have a warm-water port. With the post-war oil boom, Iran became a power in the Middle East. However, the revolution, followed immediately by the long war with Iraq, kept them isolated until recently.

MG 3

When Iran purchased Heckler & Koch G3 rifles in the early 1970s, it made sense to only purchase machine guns in the same calibre. They replaced their US .30 and .50 Brownings and the ZB 30 light machine guns they had on hand with the updated German MG42, aka the MG 3. One of the updates to the MG 3 was the ability to use disintegrating belts as well as the German continuous ones. Those machine guns no doubt went on to serve in the Iran-Iraq War in the early 1980s. The MG 3 was purchased in the early 1970s and has remained in service to the present. As they are entirely serviceable and nearly indestructible, they will probably remain in service for quite some time.

SPECIFICATION

MANUFACTURER Rheinmettal Borsig
CALIBRE 7.62mm NATO
MAGAZINE CAPACITY Belt-fed
ACTION Recoil operated
TOTAL LENGTH 1,219mm/48in
BARREL LENGTH 533mm/21in
WEIGHT UNLOADED 11.56kg/25.5lb

Pakistan

As part of the pre-war British Indian Empire, Pakistan had the same selection of rifles, machine guns, spares and training as India. After independence from India, Pakistan has had almost continual friction with its neighbour, having both the border to patrol, and its own fractious north-west provinces to oversee.

MG 1A3

SPECIFICATION

MANUFACTURER POF
CALIBRE 7.62mm NATO
MAGAZINE CAPACITY Belt-fed
ACTION Recoil operated
TOTAL LENGTH 1,219mm/48in
BARREL LENGTH 533mm/21in
WEIGHT UNLOADED 11.56kg/25.5lb

Belts
The MG 1A3 accepts disintegrating and non-disintegrating belts.

The MG 1A3 is an improved (by Germany) MG 42, built under licence from Rheinmettal. The "1" denotes conversion to the NATO standard rifle cartridge of 7.62mm NATO, while the "A3" indicates the minor changes which collectively increase durability, reliability and service life of the already exemplary design. Typically, MG 1 machine guns can be made or issued with two bolt-buffer combinations. One produces a cyclic rate of 1,100 to 1,300 rpm, while the other produces 700 to 900 rpm. The MG 1A3 has been produced in Pakistan from the mid 1950s, with manufacture continuing to the present day.

India

From a British colony to independent country, India has had a long history of martial strife and arms making. The British set up armouries in India to make British-pattern small arms for their own use. After independence, India simply kept the armouries open, while upgrading to designs it saw fit for its own needs.

BREN Model 1B

SPECIFICATION

MANUFACTURER Enfield
CALIBRE 7.62 x 51mm
MAGAZINE CAPACITY 30
ACTION Gas operated/tilting lock
TOTAL LENGTH 1,156mm/45.5in
BARREL LENGTH 635mm/25in
WEIGHT UNLOADED 10.03kg/22.12lb

As with many countries post-war, converting BREN guns from .303 to 7.62mm was an attractive proposition. For a small investment, India could keep its existing weapons going long enough to find a better replacement. It has been in use from 1953 to the present day, although all conversions were completed within a few years of the start of the process. Given the wide-open spaces of India, and the long distances from one ridgeline to another in various border skirmishes, the superb accuracy of the BREN had to be an asset. Along with the BREN, India made a copy of the MAG 58. The BREN is destined to be retired as soon as the INSAS Light Machine Gun (LMG) is fielded.

7.62mm magazines are straighter than .303 magazines

China

By the modern era, China had suffered the indignity of being apportioned between the occupying powers. Combined with internal strife from competing warlords, pre-World War II, Chinese small arms lists could only be described as "eclectic". Warlords and the central government bought arms from whomever they could or whichever sales agent offered the best bribes. What could not be bought was made. With Mauser vigorous in sales, most rifles and light and medium machine guns were chambered in 7.92 x 57mm. After the revolution, China had a huge army and People's Militia to equip. It chose Soviet-pattern weapons, built at home. The volume of its production made export an attractive prospect once the Cold War had thawed somewhat.

MG Browning

sight

condensor cap

SPECIFICATION

MANUFACTURER Colt
CALIBRE 7.92 x 57mm
MAGAZINE CAPACITY Belt-fed
ACTION Recoil operated
TOTAL LENGTH 1,041mm/41in
BARREL LENGTH 610mm/24in
WEIGHT UNLOADED 14.06kg/31lb

The Browning machine gun was a natural for the Chinese market. All it needed was a supply of barrels chambered in 7.92 x 57mm and the receiver would work forever. While making one in a local workshop would have been a daunting task, Colt found it easy to produce a model in that calibre. It was made by Colt from 1919 to 1939, and used until 1949.

VZ26 copy

SPECIFICATION

MANUFACTURER Unk
CALIBRE 7.92 x 57mm
MAGAZINE CAPACITY 20
ACTION Gas operated/tilting lock
TOTAL LENGTH 1,163mm/45.8in
BARREL LENGTH 602mm/23.7in
WEIGHT UNLOADED 9.52kg/21lb

The progenitor of the BREN, the VZ26 would have been a natural choice to copy once imported. Light, handy and reliable, it would have been the centrepiece of any warlord's armoury. While China did not have a large industrial base prior to the 1960s, it did have a lot of local armouries and workshops before World War II. The design of the VZ26 is not so complicated that it could not be copied. From its introduction in 1926 to the Communist takeover in 1949, a workshop could have produced quite a few.

Manufacturing challenges
The barrel and magazine are the two hardest parts of an automatic weapon to be made. Drilling a barrel needs costly machinery or excruciating labour and magazines must be bent out of sheet steel.

Maxim Type 24

SPECIFICATION

MANUFACTURER Various

CALIBRE 7.92 x 57 & 7.62 x 54R

MAGAZINE CAPACITY Belt-fed

ACTION Recoil operated

TOTAL LENGTH 1219mm/48in

BARREL LENGTH 605mm/23.8in

WEIGHT UNLOADED 23.8kg/52.5lb
w/o mount

Robust design
Given the lack of maintenance any weapon could expect in Chinese service, the Maxim was a good choice. Short of allowing it to rust, anyone could keep a Maxim running, once they had been given a day's instruction.

The Type 24 was both purchased from Germany, and Chinese-manufactured copies of the Maxim. The Type 24, like all Maxim-type machine guns, is heavy by the standards of today, but when reliability matters the Maxim can hardly be faulted. The originals were doubtless made in 7.92mm, but converting each to 7.62 x 54R would have been a simple operation when time for an overhaul. They were first purchased in 1924 and in use throughout the 1950s.

VZ26

SPECIFICATION

MANUFACTURER Various

CALIBRE 7.62 x 39mm

MAGAZINE CAPACITY 20

ACTION Gas operated/tilting lock

TOTAL LENGTH 1,156mm/45.5in

BARREL LENGTH 635mm/25in

WEIGHT UNLOADED 10.03kg/22.12lb

7.62 x 39mm magazines much more curved

Faced with equipping an army in the millions and a People's Militia, China sought to upgrade older weapons to the new calibre. The real problem when converting a VZ26 gun to 7.62 x 39mm is that designing and producing new magazines would have been extremely difficult. It might have done better to leave the VZ26 alone and to have simply made 7.92mm ammunition for it. The conversion was made in the early 1950s, and became instantly obsolete.

DSHK Type 54

SPECIFICATION

MANUFACTURER Various Chinese
heavy industries

CALIBRE 12.7 x 109mm

MAGAZINE CAPACITY Belt-fed

ACTION Gas operated/locking flaps

TOTAL LENGTH 1,587mm/62.5in

BARREL LENGTH 1,069mm/42.1in

WEIGHT UNLOADED 35.6kg/78.5lb

After the revolution, China made its own small arms, either based on or exact copies of Soviet designs. The DSHK Type 54 is the Soviet and Chinese heavy machine gun, chambered in the Soviet equivalent of the .50 Browning. The feed mechanism uses a sprocket, rotating the belt and cartridges to the chamber. A sprocket is more robust and less complicated than a pawl and dog-leg channel to move the belt, but a sprocket makes the receiver taller. Given even the least amount of care, the DSHK is completely reliable. It is typically manufactured with a muzzle brake that produces a ferocious back-blast. The DSHK Type 54 has been made from 1954 to the present day.

Degtyarev Type 56

This Chinese-built Soviet RPD is an air-cooled belt-fed machine gun that fills the role of the squad automatic weapon (SAW). The belt is held in a drum attached to the receiver. Belts can be used without the drum. Lacking a quick-change barrel, the gun can and will overheat if not fired with restraint. Overheating will cause myriad problems, including failure to extract or runaway firing. Otherwise the Type 56 it is quite reliable, relatively light, portable and quite formidable when used properly. In production since 1956 to the present day, it faces replacement by the new Chinese small arms family.

SPECIFICATION	
MANUFACTURER Various	
CALIBRE 7.62 x 39mm	
MAGAZINE CAPACITY Belt-fed	
ACTION Gas operated/locking flaps on bolt	
TOTAL LENGTH 1,037mm/40.8in	
BARREL LENGTH 520mm/20.8in	
WEIGHT UNLOADED 7.2kg/15.9lb w/o mount	

Chinese Type 57

anti-aircraft sights

As with so many other small arms, the Communist Chinese took advantage of the manufacturing and combat experience of their Russian counterparts. The Type 57 was simply the Goryunov SG43/SGM built in China. While it was certainly adequate as a war-time medium machine gun in World War II, by the late 1950s, it was clearly not ageing well. The Goryunov was relatively light for a medium machine gun when it was designed in 1943. By 1958, when it was adopted by the Chinese, it was portly. In addition, it could not be used without a mount, the lightest of which weighed another 20kg/44lb. Despite its age, the Type 58 served until replaced by the Type 80 in 1980.

SPECIFICATION	
MANUFACTURER Various	
CALIBRE 7.62 x 54R	
MAGAZINE CAPACITY Belt-fed	
ACTION Gas operated, side-shift bolt-lock	
TOTAL LENGTH 1120mm/44.09in	
BARREL LENGTH 720mm/28.35in	
WEIGHT UNLOADED 13.83kg/30.5lb w/o mount	

Kalashnikov Type 80

Based on the Soviet PKMC 7.62 general-purpose machine gun, the Type 80 was adopted in 1980 and issued in the early 1980s. In the Soviet

Union, the PKM replaced a slew of medium machine guns. In China, the Type 80 replaced the locally designed Type 67, which had proven less than satisfactory. Simple in design, tough as an anvil, and not requiring special alloys to be constructed, the Chinese PKM did not hurt the weapon's reputation for reliability. It was first made in 1980 and there are no plans to replace it.

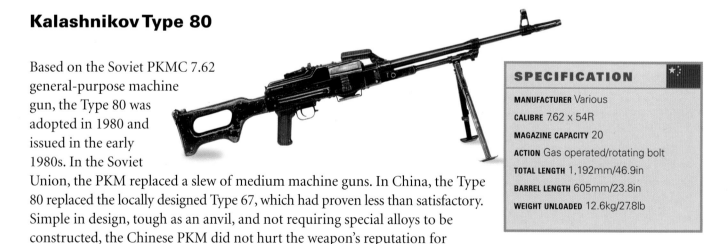

SPECIFICATION	
MANUFACTURER Various	
CALIBRE 7.62 x 54R	
MAGAZINE CAPACITY 20	
ACTION Gas operated/rotating bolt	
TOTAL LENGTH 1,192mm/46.9in	
BARREL LENGTH 605mm/23.8in	
WEIGHT UNLOADED 12.6kg/27.8lb	

 Thailand

One of the many customers of Dansk Syndikat, the Kingdom of Thailand simply bought what it needed.

In the post-war period, the US and China have been Thailand's main source of military equipment. Russia, the Czech Republic, Spain, and Sweden are its European arms suppliers.

Madsen

SPECIFICATION

MANUFACTURER Dansk Industri Syndikat
CALIBRE 7.92 x 57mm
MAGAZINE CAPACITY 30
ACTION Gas operated
TOTAL LENGTH 1,168mm/46in
BARREL LENGTH 482mm/19in
WEIGHT UNLOADED 9.97kg/22lb

This was the standard export version of the Madsen, in the standard calibre, for customers who did not insist on their own proprietary cartridge. As with all export models, customers could have their order in any calibre, kitted out with any accessories they wished. Except for the markings denoting Thai ownership, the Thai Madsen could be any other Madsen. It was in service from the 1920s, through to World War II, where it may well have been used against the Japanese.

Singapore

As a centre of heavy industry in the modern world, it has not been a problem for Singapore to invest in arms production in the modern era. Attracting designers is also straightforward. Its efforts in getting designs adopted abroad have not met with great success due mostly to the huge volume of small arms available.

CIS Ultimax 100

SPECIFICATION

MANUFACTURER Chartered Industries
  of Singapore
CALIBRE 5.56 x 45mm
MAGAZINE CAPACITY 30, 100-round drum
ACTION Gas operated
TOTAL LENGTH 1,024mm/40.31in
BARREL LENGTH 508mm/20in
WEIGHT UNLOADED 4.9kg/10.80lb

The Ultimax 100 is a Light Machine Gun (LMG) or Squad Automatic Weapon (SAW) that reduces felt recoil by a simple method: the receiver is long enough internally to prevent the cycling bolt from striking the rear of the receiver. The firer only feels the spring compression, never the bolt bottoming out against the rear of the receiver. As a result, it is very smooth in operation. Manufacture began in the early 1980s and continues to the present day. The Ultimax is a regular contender in SAW and LMG trials, but has yet to see much acceptance outside Singapore.

CIS .50

SPECIFICATION

MANUFACTURER Chartered Industries
  of Singapore
CALIBRE .50 BMG
MAGAZINE CAPACITY Belt-fed
ACTION Gas operated
TOTAL LENGTH 1,670mm/65.74in
BARREL LENGTH 1,141mm/44.92in
WEIGHT UNLOADED 30kg/66.13lb

This is another contender to try and throw the Browning M2HB off the throne. The CIS .50 has dual-feed, right and left. The feed is selectable, and the firer can switch from one to the other and use either type being fed. It is lighter than the M2HB. The barrel is a quick-change design, and the firing mechanism offers semi- and full-auto firing. The bolt rotates to lock, and features 24 small locking lugs, arranged in three rows. The advantage of such a design is that it allows for a more compact receiver, as the bolt is kept to the minimum size needed for safe function. It was introduced in the 1990s.

 # Australia

Australia did not have its own government rifle factory until the establishment of the Lithgow Arsenal in 1912. Production of Vickers began in 1925, and subsequently that of BREN guns in 1938. Once World War II was underway, the Lithgow Arsenal worked day and night to meet demand.

BREN Mark 1

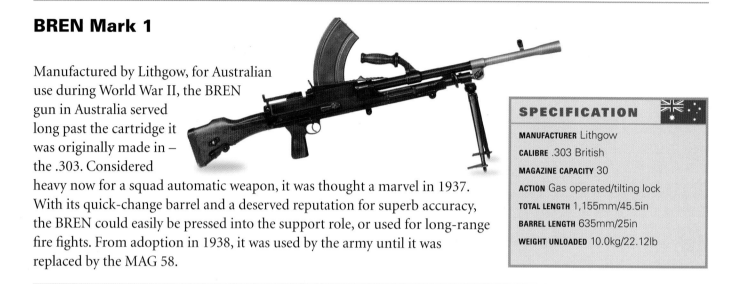

Manufactured by Lithgow, for Australian use during World War II, the BREN gun in Australia served long past the cartridge it was originally made in – the .303. Considered heavy now for a squad automatic weapon, it was thought a marvel in 1937. With its quick-change barrel and a deserved reputation for superb accuracy, the BREN could easily be pressed into the support role, or used for long-range fire fights. From adoption in 1938, it was used by the army until it was replaced by the MAG 58.

SPECIFICATION

MANUFACTURER Lithgow
CALIBRE .303 British
MAGAZINE CAPACITY 30
ACTION Gas operated/tilting lock
TOTAL LENGTH 1,155mm/45.5in
BARREL LENGTH 635mm/25in
WEIGHT UNLOADED 10.0kg/22.12lb

Vickers Mark 1

In 1925 the Lithgow plant was expanded and tooling installed to begin production of the Vickers machine gun, in addition to the manufacture of Lee-Enfield rifles. With the extra weight of the tripod (50lb), and water in the jacket, a World War I-era machine gun is not exactly a portable weapon. However, neither jungle operations nor amphibious assaults in the Pacific were exemplars of fluid warfare. A completely dependable, if heavy, machine gun, it was highly valued. It was adopted in 1925 and used (along with the BREN) until it was replaced by the MAG 58.

SPECIFICATION

MANUFACTURER Lithgow
CALIBRE .303 British
MAGAZINE CAPACITY Cloth belts
ACTION Recoil operated, water cooled
TOTAL LENGTH 1,092mm/43in
BARREL LENGTH 721mm/28.4in
WEIGHT UNLOADED 14.96kg/33lb
  w/o water

long-range sight

wood ammunition box, with 100 rounds in a belt

condenser can, to cool steam

Water-cooler can
The can that is often seen with a water-cooled machine gun is the condenser. In addition to supplying additional water for cooling, it cools and condenses the steam produced by the heat of firing. Without it, the machine gun could be quickly spotted by the plume of steam coming out of the water jacket vent.

F89

SPECIFICATION

MANUFACTURER Lithgow

CALIBRE 5.56 x 45mm NATO

MAGAZINE CAPACITY 30 and belt-fed

ACTION Gas/rotating bolt

TOTAL LENGTH 1,038mm/40.9in

BARREL LENGTH 465mm/18.3in

WEIGHT UNLOADED 6.90kg/15.2lb

This was the Australian-built version of the FN Minimi, adopted in 1989 and still in use today. The F89 has a picatinny rail on which can be mounted a 1.5 power optic sight. The combination allows a gunner to engage targets at the extreme range of the 5.56mm cartridge, and the rail allows the gunner to mount night-vision optics if necessary. The F89 uses either belted ammunition in 100 and 200-round disintegrating belts, or 30-round M-16 magazines.

North Korea

North Korea makes copies of the standard Soviet arms. The Korean People's Army (KPA) was expanded during the 1970s and 1980s from half a million men to its present size of 1.2 million men, and a force that large needs many arms. Given the extremes of climate and terrain, simple but durable guns are a wise choice.

RPD

SPECIFICATION

MANUFACTURER N. Korea Arsenal

CALIBRE 7.62 x 39mm

MAGAZINE CAPACITY Belt-fed

ACTION Gas operated

TOTAL LENGTH 1,036mm/40.8in

BARREL LENGTH 520mm/20.5in

WEIGHT UNLOADED 7.07kg/15.6lb

The quality of manufacture of North Korean small arms is reported to be quite good internally, even if the exteriors are reported to be rough. The roughness may be more a matter of a harsh service environment, and the rigours that led to their capture, than a lack of concern for exterior finish. Other than the Korean markings, this weapon is a standard RPD, with all the strengths and weaknesses of the gun. It has been manufactured from the late 1950s to the present day.

South Korea

In 1950 the North invaded, and since the stalemate of 1953 Korea has been divided between North and South. The South Korean Army is only half the size of the KPA facing it from the North, but determined to resist an invasion. Daewoo is an an industrial giant; makers of a wide variety of products besides small arms.

Daewoo K3

SPECIFICATION

MANUFACTURER Daewoo

CALIBRE 5.56 x 45mm

MAGAZINE CAPACITY M-16 magazines & belt-fed

ACTION Gas operated

TOTAL LENGTH 1,030mm/40.55in

BARREL LENGTH 533mm/21in

WEIGHT UNLOADED 6.85kg/15.10lb

An aspirant for the Squad Automatic Weapon (SAW) market and clearly inspired by the FN Minimi, the Daewoo K3 is a solid light machine gun in use by the South Korean Defence Forces. It has not yet been accepted elsewhere but, as large as Daewoo is, contending with FN is not an easy task. Issue to South Korean Army units began in 1990 and the K3 remains in service in Korea, if not elsewhere. With a quick-change barrel and able to use either belt or box magazines, the K3 would serve as well as the FN Minimi. The fact that the FN Minimi was on the market first should not be held against the K3.

Japan

Not only did Japanese machine guns use 6.5 and 7.7mm cartridges, there were further complications: some were rimmed, some were semi-rimmed, and none were interchangeable. Add to this a few foreign makes such as the Japanese-made Lewis Gun in .303 British, and the fact that the Army, Navy and Air Force selected models without consulting each other, then supplying troops with ammunition must have been very challenging.

Nambu Type 11

Another modified Hotchkiss, the Nambu Type 11 used the same 6.5mm cartridges as Japanese rifles and the same stripper clips. The feed "system" was a hopper that held the stripper clips. The operator would lift the hinged feed paddle and drop loaded stripper clips in, horizontally, and point forward. He would also have to operate the cartridge oiler. The machine gun would feed the rounds off the stripper clips, and eject empty brass and stripper clips. Contemporary shooters say that the oiler system was effective. The Type 11 was introduced in 1922 and used until 1945.

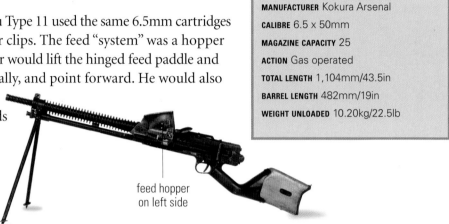

feed hopper on left side

SPECIFICATION	●
MANUFACTURER Kokura Arsenal	
CALIBRE 6.5 x 50mm	
MAGAZINE CAPACITY 25	
ACTION Gas operated	
TOTAL LENGTH 1,104mm/43.5in	
BARREL LENGTH 482mm/19in	
WEIGHT UNLOADED 10.20kg/22.5lb	

Hotchkiss-designed Type 93

Licensed from the French (who never built any), the Hotchkiss-designed Type 93 met a need the Japanese experienced after their invasion of China: long range and power. The 6.5mm machine guns that they had were not up to long-range machine gun duels, but the Type 93 with its powerful 13mm cartridge solved that problem. Built in the late 1920s and early 1930s, it was not made in particularly large numbers and served until the end of World War II.

SPECIFICATION	●
MANUFACTURER Tokyo Arsenal	
CALIBRE 13 x 99mm	
MAGAZINE CAPACITY 20-round trays	
ACTION Gas operated	
TOTAL LENGTH 2,413mm/95in	
BARREL LENGTH 1,651mm/65in	
WEIGHT UNLOADED 96.61kg/213lb w/tripod	

Lewis Type 92

96-round drum

This was a Japanese-built copy of the Lewis for flexible mounting in aircraft for use by the Japanese Imperial forces. It is not be confused with the Nambu/Hotchkiss Type 92. Curiously, the copy was also made in British .303, rather than the Japanese 7.7mm, which the Lewis mechanism could easily have handled. Consequently, the Imperial Air Force added yet another calibre to the ammunition supply chain. It was manufactured for the Air Force from 1924 until 1945.

SPECIFICATION	●
MANUFACTURER Tokyo Arsenal	
CALIBRE .303 British	
MAGAZINE CAPACITY 47- or 96-round drums	
ACTION Gas operated	
TOTAL LENGTH 940mm/37in	
BARREL LENGTH 660mm/26in	
WEIGHT UNLOADED 9.97kg/22lb	

Type 89

SPECIFICATION	●
MANUFACTURER Tokyo Arsenal	
CALIBRE 7.7 x 58mm	
MAGAZINE CAPACITY Belt-fed	
ACTION Recoil operated	
TOTAL LENGTH 1,051mm/41.4in	
BARREL LENGTH 686mm/27in	
WEIGHT UNLOADED 16.78kg/37lb	

This was a copy of the Vickers machine gun, which had a reputation for being solid and reliable. The Type 89 was close enough as to almost have interchangeable parts. It was used as an aircraft gun and also would have been pressed into use on the ground. At least infantry units using salvaged Type 89 machine guns could count on them using the standard 7.7mm rifle cartridge, as long as they saved the belts and reloaded them. It was manufactured and used from 1928 until 1945.

Type 92

SPECIFICATION	●
MANUFACTURER Tokyo Arsenal	
CALIBRE 7.7 x 58SR	
MAGAZINE CAPACITY Tray feed, 30 rounds each	
ACTION Gas operated	
TOTAL LENGTH 1,156mm/45.5in	
BARREL LENGTH 731mm/28.8in	
WEIGHT UNLOADED 28.12kg/62lb (tripod another 27.21kg/60lb)	

The Type 92 is a heavy machine gun of Hotchkiss-type design, that required a new cartridge – a semi-rimmed 7.7mm: Type 92. When a new cartridge and machine gun are introduced into service the old ones should be withdrawn. The new Type 92 ammunition was more powerful than the 7.7mm, and rifles could not fire it. Conversely, the Type 92 could fire rifle ammunition. The tripod was fitted with sections of pipe, allowing it to be carried, stretcher-like, for short distances. It was introduced in 1932 and remained in service until the end of World War II.

Nambu Type 96

SPECIFICATION	●
MANUFACTURER Tokyo Arsenal and others	
CALIBRE 6.5 x 50mm	
MAGAZINE CAPACITY 30	
ACTION Gas operated	
TOTAL LENGTH 1,054mm/41.5in	
BARREL LENGTH 552mm/21.75in	
WEIGHT UNLOADED 9.07kg/20lb	

The Type 96 is reported to be an improved Type 11, but it is simply the Czech ZB in 6.5 x 50mm, built for the Imperial Navy. Doing away with the cartridge oiler, the hopper feed of the Type 11 and changing to a quick-change barrel and magazine feed, the Type 96 is a much superior Light Machine Gun (LMG) to the Type 11. The Type 96 often had a 2.5x optical sight attached to the receiver, a first for an LMG. It entered service in 1936 and lasted until 1945.

Nambu Type 99

bayonet mounting stud

SPECIFICATION	●
MANUFACTURER Tokyo Arsenal	
CALIBRE 7.7 x 58mm (could also use 7.7 x 58SR)	
MAGAZINE CAPACITY 30	
ACTION Gas operated	
TOTAL LENGTH 1,187mm/46.75in	
BARREL LENGTH 549mm/21.6in	
WEIGHT UNLOADED 10.43kg/23lb	

This was another Czech ZB copy, in 7.7mm rimless for use at the squad level. The fact that the Type 99 looks very much like the Type 96 only increased the confusion over ammunition (and in this case, magazine) supply. The Type 99 and Type 92 both used 7.7mm ammunition, but with different rim diameters on the case heads. The Nambu Type 99 was an excellent model, but the Japanese never had enough of them. Initially built for the army, it also entered service with Naval garrison units, often mistakenly called "Marines". Production began in 1939 and lasted to 1945.

Index

PICTURE CREDITS
The publisher would like to thank the following for supplying photos for this book: AirSeaLand Photos Limited: 24, 25b, 30b, 32b, 34b, 36b, 38t; The Lordprice Collection: 11t, 14t, 34t; Peter Newark's Military Pictures: 7t, 9, 10, 11b, 13t, 16b, 28t, 37; Royal Armouries Picture Library: 22b, 33b; Will Fowler: 2, 17, 18, 25t, 27b, 28b, 29, 31b, 33t, 35, 38b, 39b.

All other images are commissioned. With thanks to the Royal Armouries, Leeds in England for allowing access to their extensive collection of firearms. All commissioned pictures by Gary Ombler. All artwork by Peters & Zabransky Ltd. Every effort has been made to acknowledge photographs correctly, however we apologize for any unintentional omissions, which will be corrected in future editions.

ABOVE Browning Mark 2, Air Service (UK).